MANY THINGS IN PARABLES

MANY THINGS IN PARABLES
Reflections for Life

JOSEPH FICHTNER, O.S.C.

ALBA · HOUSE   NEW · YORK

SOCIETY OF ST. PAUL, 2187 VICTORY BLVD., STATEN ISLAND, NEW YORK 10314

Library of Congress Cataloging-in-Publication Data

Fichtner, Joseph.
    Many things in parables: reflections for life / by Joseph
Fichtner.
       p. 157   cm. 14 × 21
       Includes index.
       ISBN 0-8189-0536-0
       1. Jesus Christ—Parables—meditations.   I. Title.
    BT375.2.F48   1988
    242'.5—dc19   88-17695
                                                                  CIP

Designed, printed and bound in the United States of
America by the Fathers and Brothers of the
Society of St. Paul, 2187 Victory Boulevard,
Staten Island, New York 10314, as part of their
communications apostolate.

Printing Information:

Current Printing - first digit   2 3 4 5 6 7 8 9 10 11 12 13 14 15 16 17 18 19 20

Year of Current Printing - first year shown
                    1990   1991   1992   1993   1994   1995   1996   1997   1998   1999

CONTENTS

PROLOGUE

In T.S. Eliot's play, *The Cocktail Party*, Julia, a character given to gossip, is asked to tell a story. "Well, one can't be too careful," she remarks, "before one tells a story."

A gossipy story can easily tell against the storyteller, if for no other reason than that its detail may be remembered against her or him. The detail may float about like bubbles in a cocktail glass, as devoid of merit as gossip itself.

The parables of Jesus announced good, heady, but not gossipy news. They were well remembered, for they had an adhesive quality of sticking to the memory. They were retold frequently but not written down until many years after his death. One has to be careful in their retelling.

Jesus narrated them in Aramaic, which flowed like Eliot's verse into poetic rhythm that glued them to the memory. Further, he spoke slowly, with emphatic pause. They contained examples to live by—religious and moral lessons. Jesus didn't always elaborate their exact applications; most often he left them to be worked out by his hearers. No wonder his stories, once fit into a cultural context, have been transmitted to us as parts of a wisdom literature.

The pastoral, rural imagery in his parables may seem foreign to a citified culture. Jesus wasn't a city-slicker. He was much more prone to paint a landscape than a cityscape. Jesus didn't travel the countryside with a candid camera handy. Nonetheless he was a careful observer of his times and places and drew word-pictures.

Most of his stories reflected himself, his character, his life and work. They "pictured" how they got him into the trouble with the religious authorities that led to his death, but, likewise, how his followers might become more Christ-like. They show his resemblance to God the Father.

Many Things in Parables went through a process similar to the stories of Jesus. They were "listened to" in as much of their spokenness as possible, then reflected on, and shared informally in a "cozy corner," with a small group. They were left in their original order of presentation, not categorized by Scriptural author or theme.

The vivid and striking pictures they convey, stir the imagination, and in so doing revive the parables, drawing us into them. They revisit us. They allow for points of view which cast them in a new light.

Set in a book form, hopefully they will continue to be remembered and put to use in the same way that the apostle Paul, relying on the oral tradition of his day, and revisiting the places of Jesus' ministry, alluded to the parables of Jesus in his preaching and teaching. Jesus would be well pleased to have the many things in his parables rehearsed in reflection, dialogue, and prayer.

Joseph Fichtner, O,S.C.

Reflections for Life

ABBREVIATIONS

OLD TESTAMENT

Genesis	Gn	Nehemiah	Ne	Baruch	Ba
Exodus	Ex	Tobit	Tb	Ezekiel	Ezk
Leviticus	Lv	Judith	Jdt	Daniel	Dn
Numbers	Nb	Esther	Est	Hosea	Ho
Deuteronomy	Dt	1 Maccabees	1 M	Joel	Jl
Joshua	Jos	2 Maccabees	2 M	Amos	Am
Judges	Jg	Job	Jb	Obadiah	Ob
Ruth	Rt	Psalms	Ps	Jonah	Jon
1 Samuel	1 S	Proverbs	Pr	Micah	Mi
2 Samuel	2 S	Ecclesiastes	Ec	Nahum	Na
1 Kings	1 K	Song of Songs	Sg	Habakkuk	Hab
2 Kings	2 K	Wisdom	Ws	Zephaniah	Zp
1 Chronicles	1 Ch	Sirach	Si	Haggai	Hg
2 Chronicles	2 Ch	Isaiah	Is	Malachi	Ml
Ezra	Ezr	Jeremiah	Jr	Zechariah	Zc
		Lamentations	Lm		

NEW TESTAMENT

Matthew	Mt	Ephesians	Ep	Hebrews	Heb
Mark	Mk	Philippians	Ph	James	Jm
Luke	Lk	Colossians	Col	1 Peter	1 P
John	Jn	1 Thessalonians	1 Th	2 Peter	2 P
Acts	Ac	2 Thessalonians	2 Th	1 John	1 Jn
Romans	Rm	1 Timothy	1 Tm	2 John	2 Jn
1 Corinthians	1 Cor	2 Timothy	2 Tm	3 John	3 Jn
2 Corinthians	2 Cor	Titus	Tt	Jude	Jude
Galatians	Gal	Philemon	Phm	Revelation	Rv

1

PARABLE OR PORTRAIT?

Mk 4:2ff.; Mt 13:3-9; Lk 8:5-8

"He taught them [a huge crowd] many things in parables.
. . . When he was alone, the Twelve, together with the others
who formed his company, asked what the parables meant. He
told them, 'The secret of the kingdom of God is given to you, but
to those who are outside everything comes in parables, so that
they may see and see again, but not perceive; may hear and hear
again, but not understand; otherwise they might be converted
and be forgiven.' He said to them, 'Do you not understand the
parable? Then how will you understand any of the parables? . . .'
Using many parables like these, he spoke the word to them, so
far as they were capable of understanding it. He would not speak
to them except in parables, but he explained everything to his
disciples when they were alone" (Mk 4:2, 10-18, 33-34).

A primitive but most human characteristic was the habit of
story-telling—everywhere and always, so far as it has been
discoverable in history. It showed traces of circumstance and
purpose, religious and instructional, among others. But ulterior
to such purposes was the delight in the story for its own sake.

The oldest style of story is the myth. Pure and simple, it's
the fabrication about the origins of our race and our world,
though not always as elaborated as we find it in the book of

Genesis. Alongside it arose Aesop's fables. Aesop, according to the historian Herodotus, was a slave who lived in the mid-sixth century before Christ, about the same time as one of the Genesis stories was circulating. But Aesop told fables for a political purpose. Grimm's fairy tales and the tales of Hans Christian Andersen, the nineteenth-century Danish storyteller, have almost the same appeal—the color, aroma, taste—as the short story and the novel. The parables of Jesus belong to this great classic literature, and excel it.

The Hebrew people of old possessed a folklore with fiction and popular stories tossed in. Probably, what was not distinctively Hebraic was the parable. The Hebrew name for it is *mashal*, a generic term for every figure of speech: metaphor, simile, allegory, fable, proverb, riddle, symbol, example, theme, etc. It's within this wider extension of the term that we should appreciate the parables of Jesus. "What a wonderful thing is metaphor" (Christopher Frye).

The parable is found already in all the Old Testament writings—historical, prophetic, wisdom, apocalyptic. But it abounds in the *Hagada* of the Talmud, the *Midrash*, and the Apocrypha (which we can classify as biblical commentaries). The latter three, owing to their nonhistorical and sometimes too fanciful import, excluded themselves from the Scripture but retained their spiritual value. Ancient custom picked up stories from the plain folk and retold them. On their way back to the people they underwent variation and adaptation. Thus they grew into an amazingly big collection.

Even so, King Solomon was credited with "inventing" the parable, supposedly because he in his wisdom was held to be the originator of wisdom literature. The parable was esteemed by the rabbis of old who taught the Talmud. It was an easy method of teaching the synagogue audience and keeping it from falling asleep. The *Hagada* valued it as follows: "Do not despise the parable. With a penny candle one may often find a lost gold coin or a costly pearl. By means of a trifling simple parable one may sometimes penetrate into the most profound ideas."

Would we Christians understand Jesus better had he left behind a portrait of himself to see and see again? Or was he prohibited by the law of Moses from making idols of God: "You shall not make yourself a carved image or any likeness of anything in heaven or on earth beneath or in the waters under the earth" (Ex 20:4)? No, instead, his stories represent God in imagery of all kinds. Everything in nature and history which he draws upon, contain his presence and power, and resemble him. Human beings especially, created by God in his image and likeness, in speaking, give voice to him. Yet nobody speaks better, more understandingly of God than Jesus, the original image and likeness of the Father and the Word of God. Yet the Chinese proverb, "One picture is worth more than ten thousand words," would have appealed to him.

His word prompts people to ponder the value and direction of human life, challenging them to come to a decision about it, and at the same time to a decision for or against himself, because the kingdom he announces originates with himself, with a word he affirms with his life.

This explains why some of his hearers don't convert and believe in him. His words prod them, pack a punch, and are so perturbing at times that his hearers turn against him. His motive isn't to send them on a guilt trip but for them to be honest and open to his preaching and teaching. Jesus isn't about to force himself or his message on them. He doesn't tell his stories to abuse or confuse "outsiders," as if they're about to be kept out of his kingdom. They're left with a freedom of choice. Apathy to or rejection of him and his message thwarts no one but oneself.

As for ourselves, to accept the gospel parables is to arrive at a better belief in Jesus and understanding, by way of reflection, of ourselves. Something of the secret of his humanity—how he's the image and likeness of God—is unveiled to us. They bring us closer in appearance to him, for as word-events they work their effects on us. A quick benefit we shouldn't expect, for they demand more than a superficial hearing, a glance, or even a slight change of heart. They're not storytelling to tickle the ear or tantalize the imagination or humor the heart. Words of wisdom, they call for close attention, wonder and reflection.

As comparisons, they have universal application, even though they're not always well understood. Unlike a picture, one parable isn't worth more than ten thousand words. Each still has an "elan vital" for every member of the human family. Each and every one of them throbs with the heart of life, its meaning.

2

MY KINGDOM FOR A...

Mk 1:15, 4:17ff.;   Mt 4:12-17;   Lk 4:14-15

Whenever we pray the Our Father Jesus taught us, it
revives a theme he preached in his parables: "Thy kingdom
come, thy will be done, on earth as it is in heaven." Praying "thy
kingdom come" helps to actualize the kingdom.

The introduction to a parable reveals its nature. Jesus
begins, "This is what the kingdom of God is like," or, "What can
we say the kingdom of God is like?" His story then develops by
way of a comparison, in the course of which he expands on the
good news of the kingdom.

Mainly, Jesus continues an Old Testament theme, defining
the divine-royal power in behalf of the people of Israel. Kingship
promises deliverance or liberation for Israel as well as for all
peoples. Psalm 68 dramatizes the stages of the royal triumph of
God, the first of which is the exodus from Egypt. Later, even
though Israel begs God for a human king, the prophet Isaiah lets
the people freed from exile in Babylonia know who their real
ruler is: "Your *God* is king!" (Is 52:7). A royal psalm that takes its
cue from Isaiah and other psalms, exhorts Israel to relay this
information: "Say among the nations, 'Yahweh is king!' " (Ps
96:10). The kingdom-theme handed down to the people of his
time was familiar and useful to Jesus. But if his early followers

7

had publicized it in the Roman Empire, it would have sounded like a threat to the emperors, something like the contemporary feeling harbored against mixing religion with politics.

The theme, "The time has come, and the kingdom of God is close at hand. Repent, and believe the Good News" (Mk 1:15), pulls together all the strands of Jesus' teaching. In addition, the evangelist Matthew makes it, in terms of the kingdom "of heaven," central to his entire gospel. He avoids "of God" in deference to the Jewish people of his day, for whom he intends his gospel and to whom the name of God is sacred beyond speech (cf. Mt 4:17).

Similarly, the word "kingdom" may sound foreign to us Americans who live in a democratic, capitalistic society, and even somewhat "hostile" inasmuch as it recalls the history of American resentment to King George III who tried to maintain English supremacy over the early American colonies. The biblical use of the Greek *basileia*, however, translates into the reign or rule of God over nature and history—over all of his creation and all of his redemptive acts. It extends not simply to a territory or to politics but to *people*. Their welfare is the first concern and care of his Royal Highness.

The hostile forces, who are allowed an evil lease on time till the end of the world, are triumphed over at last. But in the meantime Evil is competing with God and Christ for control over creation. "But if it is through the Spirit of God that I cast devils out," said Christ, "then know that the kingdom of God has overtaken you" (Mt 12:28; Lk 11:20).

That the kingdom has "overtaken" us, or is "at hand," is something new, even startling, yet meant to be part and parcel of human life, personal and social. We may pray for its coming, as if it has yet to come, while Jesus in the act of preaching already sets it up "on earth as it is in heaven." His word transforms secular history into salvation history, turning everything into the kingdom of God fully and finally only in the last times.

Time-wise, his kingdom is always in the process of realization. It already contains the meaning and value of human life, work, prayer and play, and yet there's much more to come. The date of its fulfillment is uncertain, but in our spirit of faith and hope we're assured of the fact. The kingdom has an "already/not yet" thrust to it. Earthly kingdoms come and go; the heavenly has only to come.

Most likely, were it solely a human project, a kingdom of science and technology, of human architecture and construction, or a polity, we would like to hurry it along or set a deadline for its completion. No brick-and-mortar edifice, no calendar of present or future events will inform us about how the kingdom is progressing. No camera crews will be on location to picture it for us. Essentially it's a gift of God, God acting in the single moment of time-and-eternity.

When Jesus begins to proclaim the kingdom in Palestine, some of his hearers conjure up nationalistic ideas of it. Is it any wonder? That human kingdoms—not to speak of other systems of government—have always been nationalistic or imperialistic is a fact of history. On the contrary, the divine kingdom has a universal or worldwide outreach. So when the Pharisees inquire about it, particularly the time of its arrival, Jesus' answer is: "The coming of the kingdom of God does not admit of observation and there will be no one to say, 'Look here! Look there!' For, you must know the kingdom of God is among you" (Lk 17:20-21).

If the kingdom "does not admit of observation" in our own time, among us, how are we to envision the Church vis-a-vis the kingdom? Is the Church, a visible body of people, the sacrament of the kingdom, providing signs and means to it? Is the purpose of all her ministries to build up the kingdom? Vatican II responds: "Earthly progress must be carefully distinguished from the growth of Christ's kingdom. Nevertheless, to the extent that the former can contribute to the better ordering of human society, it is of vital concern for the kingdom of God" (*Gaudium et Spes*, #39). In this faith-view, the Church is a part of and a preparation for the kingdom.

While we belong to the Church, live in the kingdom and look forward with hope to its completion, we shouldn't stand by idle, impatient, or helpless. The observance, personal and social, of truth and life, of holiness and grace, of justice, love and peace leads to the growth of the kingdom (see the Preface of the solemnity of Christ the King).

In the liturgy, indeed, at the finish of the Our Father, we pray together to the Lord and King of the universe: "For the kingdom, the power and the glory are yours, now and forever!" In answer to our prayer, only he can look on the faith of his Church and grant her the peace and unity of his kingdom.

3

ONE DEATH IS THE PARENT

Mk 4:26-29;   Mt 13:33

Here and there in the gospels parables are paired together for literary effect, even though they may have been told apart, on separate occasions. The "seed" and the "yeast" are such, the one drawn from a small Palestinian agricultural setting, the other from the daily custom of baking bread. You have to have experienced gardening or baking bread to appreciate more fully the two comparisons.

The seed symbolizes the word of God. It doesn't take much effort to understand how a word can be planted in the mind. That's precisely what Jesus intends to do—plant a word in us to make us think about the mystery of life and growth. Listening to his word, in turn, obligates us to witness to and proclaim it. Otherwise the seed grows old and sterile and the yeast loses its energy. What method, then, of evangelization are we to use so that the word will produce its full effect?

Like the harvest that's compressed in the seed, Jesus is brief in his speech and skips over details. No explanation is given of how the seed sprouts and develops at length into the harvest. More likely, Jesus wants to point up the contrast between a small start and a flourishing finish, while leaving to our imagination the paradoxical expansion or growth that lies in between.

11

First the farmer broadcasts the seed over the land, then he whiles away night and day, during which the earth produces a harvest "he knows not how." He's ignorant of the mystery of life and growth, that transformation from within, that interior change, just as we are of the divine plan and force of salvation. Once the harvest is ready, the farmer loses no time to reap it: "Put the sickle in: the harvest is ripe; come and tread, for the wine press is full," says the prophet Joel (3:13).

Left with a mystery, modern-day scientists still puzzle over the process of evolution from start to finish. But rather than theorize about it as they do, we must meditate upon the seed and yeast with a sense of wonder, the wonder that the word of God they symbolize should live and grow in our hearts and minds.

We can't easily assess growth in ourselves, in our society, or the progress of the Church toward the kingdom. Jesus, I believe, wants to alleviate or obviate disappointment at the lack of visible growth or progress in the spiritual life by telling us that, without any outward intimation of it, there's bound to be a glorious finish.

The farmer or husbandman has a *patient* faith, which keeps him from disappointment. "Think of the farmer," writes James, "how patiently he waits for the precious fruit of the ground until it has had the autumn rains and the spring rains! You too have to be patient; do not lose heart, because the Lord's coming will be soon" (5:7-8). Since it's really God "who makes things grow," the best we can do is to be co-workers with him (cf. 1 Cor 3:6, 9).

See how Emily Dickinson encapsulates the mystery of the word of God in this verse:

> A Word is dead
> When it is said,
> Some say.
> I say it just
> Begins to live
> That day.

However her verse was inspired, it relates very closely to the saying in the gospel of John: "Unless a wheat grain falls on the ground and dies, it remains only a single grain, but if it dies, it yields a rich harvest" (12:24). The paradox of death and life confronts all who listen to the word of God. As Cardinal Newman observed, "One death is the parent of a thousand lives."

We get an inkling of a tremendous rate of growth in the kingdom of God by contrasting kingship in the Old Testament, which eventually died out, with the kingdom which Christ the King announces and realizes in himself, or, by looking from his infant Church to the present stage of its development.

The yeast, the second metaphor, brings to mind my own experience of baking bread for the first time. I tried to remember how my mother did it. She followed the same process as the Israelites of old, covering the dough with a cloth and letting it rise overnight. Bulging over the pans in the morning, the dough awakened in us children a sense of mystery. That my batch of dough didn't rise much, I thought strange. But I gave it no further attention. Once the bread was baked, I saw disappointedly how flat and solid it was, rather than light and spongy. I suspected that the package of yeast which I had pulled out of the cupboard must have been too old and had lost its energy. The date on the package confirmed my suspicion.

Ordinarily yeast permeates without losing its energy, though it may signify bad will and disposition—a sour dough. "Keep your eyes open; be on your guard against the yeast of Pharisees and the yeast of Herod," warned Jesus (Mk 8:15). Paul indicates the same effect of yeast in his letter to the Corinthians: "You must know how even a small amount of yeast [the yeast of pride] is enough to leaven all the dough" (1 Cor 5:6), or to the Galatians, "The yeast [of falsehood] seems to be spreading through the whole batch of you" (5:9).

In the biblical understanding of it, leavening suggests the

idea of a limitless source of power which the word of God has in promulgating the kingdom. The *human* word of the preacher or teacher isn't powerful or persuasive enough—"the thing that you sow is not what is going to come" (1 Cor 15:37). It needs prayerful support: "Pray for us especially, asking God to show us opportunities for announcing the message and proclaiming the mystery of Christ. . . . Pray that I may proclaim it as clearly as I ought" (Col 4:3-4).

4

GOD'S FARM

Mk 4:3-9, 14-20   Mt 13:3-9, 18-23;   Lk 8:5-8, 11-15

"Imagine a sower." Is Jesus addressing us in season, seeing somebody actually sowing grain, or out of season?

Imagine a freshly plowed field in late fall or early spring. On Wisconsin farms the soil appears a rich reddish, brown, or black color. You get a whiff of the new, upturned good earth; it exhales a feeling of springtime and may even inspire spring fever.

Then turn from a contemplation of this kind of field to another, in Palestine. There the field is unplowed, people have trod a path or paths through it, here and there rocky ground or limestone rises through, and thorns and stubble have been growing out of it. The farmer broadcasts the seed atop the earth before he plows it under. Planting precedes plowing in Palestine.

That's why seed sprays on pathways, rocky ground, among thorns, and on good earth. Consequently the farmer suffers a large loss of seed and labor.

As the story of the sower proceeds, we begin to note that it's more elaborate than a parable. It's an allegory, which has more than one point of comparison.

The seed is either the word (Mark), or the word of the kingdom (Matthew), or the word of God (Luke). In any case, it's

15

planted within the tradition of Old Testament prophetic literature, especially in the Isaian sense of the word: ". . . As the rain
and the snow come down from the heavens and do not return
without watering the earth, making it yield and giving growth to
provide seed for the sower and bread for the eating, so the word
that goes from my mouth does not return to me empty, without
carrying out my will and succeeding in what it was sent to do" (Is
55:10-11). The seed lying in the ground is, beyond doubt, fertile
and fruitful.

The sower in the story—his or her identity may vary
according to historical circumstance. In the original setting the
sower is the storyteller himself, Jesus. Crowds flock to hear him,
for he's speaking like a prophet, with authority, and questioning
them about his identity. Is Jesus he who is to come, the Messiah,
or should they look for another? Are the claims to his mission
true? How is the kingdom to come? Can his word and work really
bring about the kingdom? And where did he get all this?
Notwithstanding his authoritative voice, his preaching and
teaching seem to be ineffectual. What results do they show?

Or should we seek an explanation from the apostolic
preaching in the early Church? But its first three "soil tests" lack
something or other. Satan mingles with people on the pathways
of life, steals the word from them, depriving them of spiritual
growth. When the test of faith gets tough for the early Christians, some who are happy to hear the good news of Christianity
can't bear up under trial and persecution, so they turn into
dropouts or fallen-aways. Others run into thorny problems
causing them worry, or they're lured away by an easy, rich life
and "all the other passions come in to choke" the Christian life
out of them. That's how it goes in life for all but those who
compare well with good earth, rich soil.

The story which the early Church saw fit to accept and
appropriate to its own time, is just as applicable to us today. Like
sowers of seed, we're all called to be preachers and teachers of

the word of God. Our agricultural custom is to plow before planting, which requires that the soil of our own selves be readied for the word. Do we let it first penetrate into the witness and service of our life and into our speech? We have to ask ourselves how the seed of the blood of Christians tests out (cf. Tertullian's *Apology*, c. 21). Is it apt to bear a bumper crop?

In the original account, the rich soil (the people who hear, accept and understand the word) yields a harvest beyond expectations. For Palestinian soil to produce tenfold is an abundant harvest. But the yield, measured by near-geometric progression, 30-60-100-fold, stands for the divine blessings which not only surpass hope and prayer but overcome all the frustrations, obstacles and reversals of Christian ministry. Who would think the kingdom of God to be as universal as Jesus claims it to be?

As we come to its end, we realize ours is a success story, the kind that may have great appeal to the American farmer but still has to evangelize the people who live on God's farm. It speaks encouragingly to all who are comparable to rich soil but need a truer understanding of the means to success. Paul lays them out in his letter to the Corinthians:

> I did the planting, Apollos did the watering, but God made things grow. Neither the planter nor the waterer matters: only God, who makes things grow. It is all one who does the planting and who does the watering, and each will duly be paid according to his share in the work. We are fellow workers with God; you are God's farm . . . (1 Cor 3:6-9).

Pope Paul VI, the apostle's namesake, in his apostolic exhortation, "On Evangelization in the Modern World," outlined two ways of evangelizing. The initial way is a "wordless witness," which is "already a silent proclamation of the Good News and a very powerful and effective one" (#22). For the spread of the kingdom within his lifetime, Jesus combined witness with word and work.

Pope Paul VI saw with what hardship the seed of the word now has to contend with the cluttered field of modern communication. But he did not hesitate or doubt its efficacy: "The fatigue produced these days by so much empty talk and the relevance of many other forms of communication must not however diminish the permanent power of the word, or cause a loss of confidence in it. The word remains ever relevant, especially when it is the bearer of the power of God" (#42).

In and out of season, Jesus is still planting his word, reaping the mysteries of the Christian harvest (cf. Ps 78:2; Mt 13:35).

5

THE CHURCH OF THE POOR

Mk 12:1-11   Mt 21:33-44;   Lk 20:9-18

The tenant farmers attempt to rob an absentee landlord of his vineyard. Their plot of mistreatment and murder is a flashback to a poem by the prophet Isaiah (5:1-7): "Let me sing to my friend the song of love for his vineyard." The prophet dramatically narrates how his friend sets up a vineyard, plants it with choice vines to grow a fine-quality red grape. But, at harvest time, it disappoints him with a yield of sour grapes.

The vineyard in the Isaian poem is the house of Israel which belongs to Yahweh, who expects Israel to do right by him and remain in his favor. Instead the people get involved in bloodshed, cry out in distress and shed bitter tears.

The New Testament tale of the tenant farmers is set against the social, economic, political background of Galilee, and its plot too is full of conflict. It backtracks to some historical events and figures but it also tells the plight of the present time Galilean peasants, the poor of the land, and their revolt against foreign and absentee landlords. It keeps abreast of the Zealot movement in Galilee, which protests against Roman occupation and domination. Similarly, developing nations nowadays justly resent First World countries exploiting their natural resources without due return to their own people.

19

As the tale has come down through the synoptic writers, it shows signs of the editing one discovers in allegory. It's quite natural for storytellers to take license in the retelling of a story.

How are the details to be filled in? Well, the vineyard again represents Israel, whose owner is God. The servants or agents he sends are the prophets who are to collect his share of the produce. Evidently the tenant farmers become greedily discontent with the rent or sharecropping. They resort to violence and land seizure stirring up all kinds of social, economic, political unrest and revolution.

The mistreatment of the servants or agents at the hands of the tenant farmers worsens each time they arrive. Pre-exilic and post-exilic prophets were manhandled, even killed, for trying to keep Israel in line with the will of God. Recall Amos, Isaiah, Jeremiah, Ezekiel, Daniel (in the lion's den).

Finally, the showdown. The landlord sends his son, expecting him to be met with respect. But he's treated even worse than the rest. The tenant farmers reason that with the landlord's son out of the way, the property will, without any claims to it, revert to them. What they don't reckon with, however, is that the landlord still has the upperhand.

Throughout salvation history, Israel is the vineyard God favors, from which he expects a rich crop. The tenant farmers— the religious rulers and leaders who are to guide and teach Israel— betray it. It meets its fate in the year 70 A.D., when the Romans level Jerusalem and subdue the entire nation scattering its inhabitants to every corner of the empire.

Jesus' story concludes with a warning to contemporary Israelite leaders. They feel incriminated. Therefore they would like to be rid of the storyteller but fear the crowds who follow him.

The identity of the landlord's son is only hinted at, but it doesn't take much historical insight to see that he is Jesus himself. The fact that the son is thrown out of the vineyard first and then killed (outside Jerusalem), affords a clue about him. That he's the "beloved" son suggests the same thing (see Ac 4:11 and 1 P 2:7). Is Jesus, therefore, anticipating his own death at the hands of the Jewish leaders? He is unquestionably referring to himself as the keystone of society whom its policy makers reject (cf. Ps 118:22-23).

Now that the landlord has lost both his servants and son, he leaves his vineyard to "others." Who are they but the poor, the outcasts of society, the so-called "marginalized"? Since not enough people look after them, tend to their rights and needs, God pays them special love and attention.

In transposing this story to our life situation we're to think of the Church as the vineyard. The poor to whom God leaves his vineyard are the Africans, Asiatics, Latin Americans, among others. Liberation theology has them in mind and is trying to find ways and means of lifting them out of their social, economic, and political plight.

The new Israel, the Church, is said by Vatican II to have been "cultivated by the heavenly Vinedresser as his choice vineyard" (*Lumen Gentium*, #6). How much better or worse does the new Israel fare than the old? For the Church to promote a better order of social justice and peace, she will have to outdo the Hebrew people of the Old Testament, for they too sought such an order, though their prophets were pessimistic about its prospects. In the belief of Israel and of the Church, God alone can attain justice and peace, but only with the cooperation of people of good heart and will.

Jesus raises the question of social justice in the Galilean situation of his time. He also challenges the Church today with the need to work at a social, economic, and political renewal of society.

In his speech at Medellin, Pope John Paul II brings us up to date about social justice: "Making this world more just means . . . that there be no more peasants without land so that they can live

and develop with dignity, that there be no more workers mis-
treated nor whose rights are lessened, that there be no more
systems which permit the exploitation of man by man or by the
state . . . there be no more who have too much left over, while
others are lacking everything through no fault of their own. . . ."
They are the "others" to whom God would leave his vineyard.

6

A CHURCH UNDER CONSTRUCTION

Mt 7:24-27; Lk 6:47-49

Many of the stories in the Old Testament and in rabbinic literature are akin to the parables of Jesus. The following rabbinic story is similar to his of the two builders:

He whose wisdom exceeds his works, to what may he be likened? To a tree whose branches are numerous but whose roots are few. The wind comes along and uproots it and sweeps it down. . . . But he whose works exceed his wisdom, to what may he be likened? To a tree whose branches are few but whose roots are numerous. Then even if all the winds of the world come along and blow against it they cannot stir it from its place. . . .

Works possibly do exceed wisdom, as the rabbi discovers, if they're based on solid belief. Such a possibility occurs in the life of the Christian whose works are rooted in strong belief but who may have no deep understanding or explanation of it. The only difference then between the storytelling of Jesus and of the rabbi is that the latter exaggerates the winds that blow destructively in the world.

23

Jesus' story is placed at the end of the Sermon on the Mount, a title taken from his preaching on a hill near Capernaum. Running from chapter five through seven in the gospel of Matthew, the Sermon probably is a collection of several of Jesus' sayings about the moral qualifications for active membership in his kingdom. You may recall that it opens with the eight beatitudes that challenge Christians to the utmost but raise them to the height of sanctity. It closes on an eschatological note—the inescapable final judgment. People may shirk the dictates of their conscience during life, but that evasion only renders the final judgment more ominous.

In his preaching Jesus lays down the requirement for ministry or service in his Church. It's not a matter of saying, "Lord, Lord," nor of pronouncing the name of Jesus, nor of speaking in his name, nor of just listening to his words. Unequivocally it's a call to *action*.

Two builders are contracted: one constructs his house on rocks, the other on sand. Jesus indicates not only the kinds of foundation they build upon but the time it takes to lay the foundations. The more demanding construction on rock lasts longer even in the face of rains, floods, and wind.

The wise listen to the word of God as Jesus speaks it and they act on it. The foolish only listen. They let it go in one ear and out the other. True, firm, and lasting commitment to action perseveres through the trials and hardships every Christian encounters. Jesus taught this discipline with impressive authority, unlike the Scribes and Pharisees who relied on the tradition of their forebears.

The comparison of myself to a contractor or builder may seem far-fetched, but it points me to a personal examination. How do I listen to the word of God and put it into action? Is there any gap between my listening and acting personally, any lag in my Christian response? I may be likelier to construct on sand rather than on rock, cutting down effort and trying to get by.

There is also the community of the Church—the house of God—to consider, and my part in it. "You are part of a building that has the apostles and prophets for its foundation, and Christ Jesus himself for its main cornerstone" (Ep 2:20). "Everyone doing the building must work carefully. For the foundation, nobody can lay any other than the one which has already been laid, that is Jesus Christ. On this foundation you can build in gold, silver and jewels, or in wood, grass and straw, but whatever the material, the work of each builder is going to be clearly revealed when the day comes. That day will begin with fire, and the fire will test the quality of each man's work. If his structure stands up to it, he will get his wages; if it is burnt down, he will be the loser, and though he is saved himself, it will be as one who has gone through fire" (1 Cor 3:10-15). It's interesting to note that St. Paul changes the imagery of the trials and hardships to fire. Fire, or rain, flood, and wind—they all constitute outside pressures on the ministry.

Through active ministry clergy, religious and laity make common cause for the construction of the Church. More activity is necessary in the Church today because of the better consciousness of the nature of the Church and a new experience of her time and place in the world. The Christian consciousness today is of a Church in a world more secularized (politically, socially, economically, culturally).

Art and architecture, for example, supply the building blocks of the "new secular religion." For the exhibition of the Vatican art collection in New York City some years ago, the occasion was celebrated with a formal dinner. Ironically, the high priests and priestesses of art resented the Catholic guests who had arranged for the exhibit. Art critics and dealers whispered to one another, "Who are these unbelievable people?" By donating money preferably for art and architecture, the rich patrons at the banquet were sponsoring the spread of the "new secular religion."

Has the foundation of the house of God, the Church, been laid once and for all in the past, on rock, or is it an ongoing task? "The Church is not truly founded," answers Vatican II, "it does not fully live, nor is it a perfect sign of Christ among men, unless along with the hierarchy a genuine laity is present and at work" (*Ad Gentes*, #21). Wisdom indeed engages all as partners in the ministry of Christ, to work upon the foundation.

The possibility for the founding of the contemporary Church, what is it? It's the penetration of the hard surface of the world, the temporal order, with the spirit of the gospel, especially the beatitudes. This task is left to the laity in particular, for they're capable and competent to be present and at work where the ground is broken for the Church of Christ. The Church "civilizes by preaching the gospel" (Pius XI). The rain, flood, wind, yes, and fire will test ministry and civilization.

7

LOST-AND- FOUND

Lk 15:3-7, 8-10;   Mt 18:12-14

"Finders keepers, losers weepers," we used to chant glee-
fully as children, rejoicing over our find because with a childlike
sense of justice we felt it was ours. Bringing back that sense of
justice and joy, Jesus combines the examples of the lost sheep
and the lost coin.

Before we listen to him (preferably we should read his
examples aloud, even to ourselves), we should note that they are
heard by two audiences, one in the Lukan version, another in the
Matthean. Audiences are crucial to the understanding of gospel
parables. In Luke it's the Scribes and Pharisees who draw Jesus'
attention. In Matthew the disciples are his audience. In both
instances Jesus is facing up to religious leaders.

Jesus wants to answer the Scribes and Pharisees' objection
to the company he keeps or allows. Why are they objecting? Do
they see themselves losing out to him? Are they jealous of his
power of attraction? Are they hypocritical in their high opinion
of themselves? Evidently their intent is to appear respectable—
respectability passes for religion, and, to this extent they deem
themselves in good standing with God. Or are they too proud to
associate with the poor? They complain that Jesus allows tax
collectors and sinners in his company. Not only does he associate

with them; he even eats with them, which is the worst kind of scandal. They are sinners and are to be kept outcasts of society.

The lost-sheep example has a man, a shepherd, as the main character. The lost-coin example features a woman in the leading role. Possibly the two represent, respectively, the rich and the poor. But possibly not, for neither of the two appears to be rich.

Jesus begins with an inquiry: "Tell me. Suppose a man" . . . "What man among you" . . . Or again, "What woman? . . ." His introduction pinpoints his purpose, which simply isn't to entertain or catch the curiosity but to make an audience think seriously about matters of life and death.

Sheep are usually counted toward evening, before nightfall, after they are herded together. A lost sheep, one out of a hundred, may not be so very valuable, but since this flock is only medium-sized—flocks run from 20 (a small flock) to 300 (a very large flock)—the owner himself has to search for the lost sheep. He can afford no hired hands. The rest of the sheep can't be left unattended but in the care of other shepherds, or they are led into a cave. Meanwhile, the lost sheep can't fend for itself. It lies down, immobile, helpless. It has to be sought, picked up, swung over the shoulders and around the neck of the shepherd, so that if necessary he can hold its feet in front of himself.

Shepherds as a lot are reputed to be dishonest. They're accused of grazing on property not their own and stealing sheep. Jesus, however, gives no hint of bad reputation. To him the shepherd represents God in search of the lost sinner. Indeed the Matthean version emphasizes the shepherd's persistent pursuit of his sheep, which tells us something about the inability of a lost sinner to return to God by his/her own willpower. The sinner is offered much encouragement by the gift of divine mercy. The lapsed Catholic is welcomed back to the Church.

Apparently the woman who has lost a coin, one out of ten, is poor. One has to peer inside her home to realize how poor she is. It consists of a windowless room, with a low door and stone floor. So poorly lit is it that she has to light a candle and sweep with a broom to hear the tinkle of the coin as it rolls across the stone floor. The coin fell from her headdress, a precious ornament. Once she recovers it, she invites her friends and neighbors in to rejoice with her.

Though the conclusions of the two versions vary somewhat, both clarify what happens when God recovers a lost sinner or anyone fallen away from the faith. Matthew remarks that God the Father doesn't want a single sinner to be lost. Luke describes how heaven rejoices over the return of the sinner. No earthly joy can compare with the heavenly. God himself delights in his power to forgive and the occasions when he uses that power. Mercy betokens the coming of his heavenly kingdom.

When we contrast the moral of the two stories—the joy at the homecoming of a sinner—with the attitude of the Pharisees and Scribes toward Jesus and his "bad" companionship, what other explanation can be offered for his conduct than that of God toward sinners? His example is his answer to his critics, the hypocritical religious leaders.

"Reconciliation and Penance," an apostolic exhortation Pope John Paul II signed on December 2, 1984, sums up the sixth general assembly of the Roman Synod of Bishops and represents the theme of the Jubilee Year, the 1950th anniversary of the Redemption. This document points to the divisions in the world and their cause, sin. Sin is alienation, lapse, the state of being lost, like a lost sheep or coin. The remedy to division is reconciliation and penance, the spirit of which only divine mercy can infuse in hearts open to it. "Penance," the pope writes, "is therefore *a conversion that passes from the heart to deeds*, and then to the Christian's whole life" (#4). Does the papal appeal touch our hearts or pass us by like an item in the lost-and-found column of the newspaper?

The return of the lost sheep to the fold of the Church is an act of reconciliation, "a *gift of God*, and *initiative on his part*" (#7). According to the apostle Paul, God was in Christ reconciling the world to himself (cf. Rm 5:10f.; Col 1:20-22).

God, rich in mercy, distributes to the Church this gift, "the great sacrament of reconciliation." Christ acts in this sacrament to gather the Church of sinners. Whenever and wherever in the world the sense of sin has been lost, with no sense of being lost, and the sacrament of penance is in crisis, Christ like a shepherd searches for lost sheep, like a woman for a lost coin, and finds them. The rite of reconciliation contains his invitation to return to a merciful God. Sadly, there was "a time for losing"; happily, a time has arrived "for searching" (Pr 3:6).

8

INVITATION TO A FEAST

Lk 14:15-24;   Mt 22:1-10

An invitation is taken to be a friendly, polite, even com-
plimentary request to attend a dinner, wedding, birthday, anniversary celebration—in short, a pleasurable event. Ordinarily
we aren't *invited* to a hospitalization or a funeral, though we may
be notified of it. So our first response is to accept an invitation
gladly, if at all possible. Refusal may seem like a breach of
etiquette, or more like a neglect of friendship.

About one such invitation to a meal, Jesus, while sitting at
table, tells of a host who sent out invitations for a nuptial banquet
or feast. The host may have been a king (he is in the Matthean
version), who wanted to celebrate for the sake of his son. After
the festivity, somebody still in the glow of the excitement,
remarked, "Happy the man who will be at the feast in the
kingdom of God!"

In reality, the nuptial invitation *is* to the feast in the
kingdom of God, for the host is God the Father, the son is the
Messiah, and the marriage is the covenant between God and his
people.

As often as the Scriptures describe the kingdom to come,
it's in terms of a banquet where the guests eat and drink together
and bask in congenial company. Feasting together is one of the

31

legitimate pleasures of life, and the banquet table affords a pleasant setting, lending itself to lively conversation.

The guest list for this nuptial event seems to start with the well-to-do, the large landowners who are expected to come formally dressed. The host invites "a large number" to display his generosity and hospitality. He spares no expense for the occasion. The custom among the upper crust of Jerusalem society is to extend a second invitation, out of courtesy, to inform the guests that the dinner is ready.

The last minute refusal of the invitation is most reprehensible. The guests either offer excuses or show no interest. What keeps them away is essentially matters of self-interest. They're too busy with new land, new cattle, a new wife, to take time off. Business before pleasure. They're the business-minded men and women and newlyweds too engrossed in their own affairs to pay attention to anyone else's. Matthew sadly points out that they mistreat and murder the servants who personally hand them a second summons.

Their refusal is remedied with the replacement of guests of lower social rank. The host won't be rebuffed and let his banquet go to waste. He keeps his second list limited to city dwellers— the poor, maimed, blind, lame—possibly the inner-city folk for whom he has no compassion, whom he invites out of no religious or altruistic motive but to mollify himself, because he's angry with the rest of society. The poorest of the poor file into the banquet hall, the homeless are given a temporary shelter.

And still there's room for banqueters. Messengers go out again, now to the city outskirts, the highways and hedgerows. Nothing is left of the free and gracious invitation. Others are herded in. They have no choice. Once the hall is full, that is, once no room is left in the kingdom of God, the original guests stand no chance of entry. The good and the bad replace them.

Originally Jesus remonstrated with his critics and opponents, the religious leaders who weren't on the guest list. Full of complaints that he ate with publicans and sinners, why should they accept or even be sent an invitation? The party host would hardly list those who declined to sit at the same table with social outcasts!

As we continue to fuse the two versions, the Lukan and the Matthean, we find that Matthew uses allegory to sketch a history of salvation up to the last judgment. It begins with the city-states of Israel. The "feast," a common Hebraic figure of speech for the kingdom of heaven, is the messianic banquet of salvation. An old figure, it still makes good sense to us who love food and drink and congenial company.

The banquet invitation passes in the course of salvation history from the Jewish leaders to the poor (Luke), or from the Jews to the Gentiles (Matthew). Starting with the prophets, the span of this history runs to the apostles, then to the Gentiles. Among the historical events, Matthew hints at the destruction of Jerusalem and its inhabitants in 70 A.D. The last episode is the entry into the banquet hall, which baptism makes possible for Christians. We have to wait a spell yet to learn what happens at the last judgment.

A second look at the royal servants sent out more than once, and we begin to see that theirs is a missionary effort. They go beyond the borders of Israel to issue a call to the Gentiles. That's how the royal servants justify the preaching of the gospel to the poor of the world.

There's no mention of the time element here, as in history, but you can easily imagine how long it must have taken to receive the refusals, to send out the second summons and then collect all the people. And think of the servants, of their mistreatment and murder. The banquet then appears to have been a drawn-out affair, centuries-long.

Yet, paradoxically, that's not the immediate impression Jesus would like to leave. He says explicitly, "Come along: everything is ready now." We're to rise to the occasion and rejoice in the fact that the kingdom is at hand. "Well, now is the favorable time; this is the day of salvation" is how Paul relays the idea of readiness to his Corinthians (2 Cor 6:2).

The invitation to the royal banquet was formally communicated to us first at our Christian baptism, directly from God, with parents and godparents at hand. His invitation is very special, unlike any other kind, which is enough to cause us to pause over his generosity. It's his free choice of guests, the banquet an initiative of his. The only sensible response has to be an act of faith and obedience and gratitude.

If left unanswered, God never follows up an invitation with undue pressure. He awaits a reply with loving kindness. His guests are always free to accept or decline in the course of salvation history.

9

R.S.V.P.

Mt 22:1-14

The "wedding garment" is stylized in the Christian tradition like an R.S.V.P. initialed on an invitation card. At the feast, remember, the king opens the banquet hall to all comers, indiscriminately. Why then should he object to the presence of a single person who appears without formal attire, especially when he has just been hustled in from the streets? Doesn't the summons to attend the party catch the man by surprise, or is he a party pooper? Should he be *expected* to get dolled up for the occasion? Is the king offended at seeing someone wearing common, everyday clothes? Or is the man silent, a dumb fool because he has crashed the party? To give definite answers to such questions is difficult.

Have you ever been stopped short by a sign posted on a restaurant door which read, "No shirt, no shoes, no service"? Or been denied entrance to a fancy restaurant for not wearing a dinner jacket? Or been asked to leave the tennis court of a country club when not playing in white tennis togs? If so, you probably felt a sense of exclusion, of ostracism, for no other reason than propriety in dress.

In trying to understand the biblical situation, we ought to know that, while a change of clothing was customarily called for in *early* Hebrew culture, it was unlikely at the time of Jesus. Some other reason must account for the exclusion of the man without proper dress.

In accordance with Hebrew custom and culture, the Bible—and Matthew in particular—regard dress to be indicative of character.

The prophet Isaiah rejoices in the Lord for clothing him "in the garments of salvation" and wrapping him "in the cloak of integrity" (61:10). "Wear white all the time, do not stint your head of oil," the wise man says, most probably to avoid summer heat and sunstroke (Ec 9:8). The apocalyptic writer sees in a vision some members of the Church of Sardis ready for entry with Christ into the heavenly kingdom. Why ready? Because they "have kept their robes from being dirtied, and they are fit to come with me, dressed in white. Those who prove victorious will be dressed, like these, in white robes" which symbolize purity, joy, victory—gifts of God (Rv 3:4-5; cf. 19:8, 22:14). Clothes, then, in the biblical sense, do more than signify style; they symbolize traits of character.

Interestingly, the king personifying God the Father, doesn't partake of the banquet but only appears during it. The banquet itself celebrates the messianic era, a time of great blessing. Jesus the Messiah compares fitness for the messianic era to a new garment (Mk 2:21). He asks his apostles to make ready for the Last Supper, celebrates it with them and remains with us in the Eucharistic memorial. But he says of himself, "I shall not eat it again until it is fulfilled in the kingdom to come" (Lk 22:16). Like the king (God), Jesus is present in the Eucharist but doesn't eat with us during the messianic era.

This era, prolonged like a Flemish feast, courses through history up to the last judgment. Just as mere presence at the king's banquet for his son doesn't suffice for the man without a "tuxedo," so mere membership in the Church doesn't qualify anyone for entry into the kingdom of heaven. We must be dressed in the clean, fresh robe of personal responsibility for our actions (*respondez-vous*), clothed with the works of faith, adorned with neighborly acts of love. When God calls us to a banquet, he doesn't excuse us from the moral responsibility of human conduct. No one is so assured of salvation, saved, as to be relieved of the personal obligation of a wedding garment, which distinguishes all who are "chosen" for the eternal banquet.

As the king steps into the hall and passes judgment on the man without a tuxedo, and has him bounced out, so God the Father, whose sovereignty is over all his creation, passes judgment on every creature. The divine command is futile without the right to pass judgment and impose sanction. Although God is sometimes represented in the Scriptures as judge of the world, more usually it is Christ who has to discharge that duty on the basis of love. While in the Old Testament the positive signs of divine judgment were prosperity, posterity and longevity, in the New the preliminary judgment at death, and the final judgment at the end of time, will rest on love of God and of neighbor. The final judgment will only reaffirm and corroborate the earlier judgment. It won't reverse it like a change of garment.

How Christ figures in the ongoing judgment is well described by Romano Guardini in his book *The Last Things*: "The doctrine of the Last Judgment is, at bottom, a revelation of Christ. . . . It implies seeing Christ in everything, carrying His image in our hearts with such intensity that it lifts us above the world, above history and the works of man, and enables us to see those things for what they are, to weigh them and assign to them their eternal value, in a word, to be their judges."

The Bible *passim* refers to the fire blazing at the end of time, prior to the final judgment. The fire of that judgment is Jesus himself inasmuch as we have the standard of his life to judge ourselves by.

Each moment of life is a time of judgment or decision—for or against Christ. That's how one gradually develops a conscience which rejects or accepts Christ who eventually decides our destiny. Christ is the judge, therefore, of the *living* and the *dead*. The final day of judgment is the day of the Son of God.

Dressing up or not for the royal banquet at the end of time is a matter of conscientious judgment. The divine judgment announced in biblical tradition isn't imposed on us from without but from within the personal conscience under God, an interior act. Conscience spells out the consequences of human conduct toward God and neighbor. If God seems angry or to have it "in" for us, or finally excludes us from the royal banquet, it connotes his respect for our freedom to dress as we like, leaving us to the disastrous outcome of personal choice and behavior (*s'il vous plait*).

The royal garment is designed with truth and life, holiness and grace, justice, love and peace. It reveals Christ.

10

THE HAPPY SERVANT

Mt 24:45-51;   Lk 12:42-46

An Old Testament proverb reads, "A clever servant enjoys the favor of the king, he uses his shrewdness to avoid disgrace" (Pr 14:35).

Belonging as it does to wisdom literature with its practical-minded advice about human life, this proverb is a kind of introduction to the parable of the wise and faithful servant or steward.

Jesus starts an important issue, the use of authority, with a question in order to provoke thought, dialogue, and decision. He queries all religious leaders but most especially his disciples (or apostles, in the Lukan text) about the sort of leadership proper for his Church. His question is apropos to all the debate about leadership in the Church since Vatican II.

Jesus outlines two modes of behavior possible to the household servant: the one wise and faithful, the other dishonest and unfaithful. The servant is endowed in his master's absence with a trust he can either keep or squander. The trust is no trifling matter, as though the master is arbitrarily inventing a responsibility. It is a matter of life or death: the provision of food which everybody needs, for the servant himself and his fellow servants, male and female (according to Luke, who never forgets the

39

ladies). The servant ought to bear the grave responsibility with wisdom and fidelity.

The master's late return is essential to the story, like the delay of the parousia. Because, while the servant not only betrays the trust—living it up, carousing, eating and drinking—he usurps authority by so oppressing and terrorizing his fellow servants as to prevent them from doing their duty conscientiously. He is guilty not only of self-indulgence but of social injustice as well.

After God chose a people to covenant with, he wished or consented to their having leaders: judges, kings, priests, prophets. The judges in particular were seated with a military-judicial trust, "to administer an impartial judgment on the people." They were under orders, "Strict justice must be your ideal, so that you may live in rightful possession of the land that Yahweh your God is giving you" (Dt 16:18, 20). They were to imitate the servant-lawgivers Moses and Joshua (Nb 12:7), or the prophets (2 K 17:13). To put their duty succinctly, they were to be "servants of God" for his people.

Accordingly, Jesus sounds a powerful warning against *abuse* of authority. Under his new covenant, the priests, Scribes and Pharisees, and all religious leaders are authorized with the keys of the kingdom of heaven. Should they betray that trust, autocratically locking others out of the kingdom, they would be held responsible. Luke seems to emphasize the fact of the greater the responsibility, the more severe the judgment. Jesus speaks from experience: his life situation brings him into conflict with religious leaders.

In the era of the Church—the era between now and the "day of the Lord" (the *parousia*)—what Paul prescribed for the Corinthian Church holds for present-day Church leaders: "People must think of us as Christ's servants, stewards entrusted with the mysteries of Christ. What is expected of stewards is that each one should be found worthy of his trust." It didn't worry

Paul whether he was found worthy or not by humans, for the Lord alone was his judge, who postpones judgment till the parousia: "There must be no passing of premature judgment" (1 Cor 4:1-2, 5).

Present-day Church authority, what it is, who has it, and what are its ranks, has been subject to review and revision. At the mention of the word "authority," we're likely to think of power. The term doesn't denote the idea of trust as it did in the instruction of Jesus. The Greek New Testament term for it is *diakonia* = service, the duty and work of a servant or steward who is in charge of the household of the faith, the Church.

That Jesus himself, the Suffering Servant, held power, and that he conferred it on leaders in his Church, is evident from the New Testament. He designated ecclesiastical power for the sake of service, hence more power should offer more service. That's why today yet, the pope, the visible head of the Church, calls himself the "servant of the servants of God," to suit himself to a servant Church. In it, everyone else too is called to be a servant, to save all people.

The two dangers always confronting the Church are, first, a type of anarchy or liberal democracy wherein God's people arrogate power to themselves, to be served rather than to serve. The second danger crops up when the Church yields to the secularization of her power. To succumb to the use of power without service is authoritarian legalism. Authority in the Church doesn't legitimately hold sway *over* the Church but offers service within her ranks, a service motivated by faith and love. Leadership in the Church, then, is equivalent to servant-hood, given in trust. It never claims a right to self-aggrandizement or promotion.

What's true of leadership in the Church is valid for government in the world. In Judaism God and world weren't sharply differentiated. Nowadays, the American bishops in their pastoral letter on Catholic social teaching and the U.S. economy reassert that the world and its resources belong to God. God chose humans who live in the world to be its stewards, to be in his employment. They have no right to monopolize, waste, or exploit his world and its goods. It's theirs only in trust; they have to prove themselves to God as his trustworthy servants. The pastoral letter reads appropriately: "God is the only real owner; human beings are the trustees of the goods given them."

As caretakers whether of the Church or of the world—both belong to God—they have a responsibility toward their Master and fellow servants. Oh, for the wisdom and fidelity to carry out that God-given trust: "Happy that servant. . . ."

11

A FAITH INVESTMENT

Mt 25:14-30;   Lk 19:11-27

The theme of the talents or pounds, though the same in Matthew and Luke, isn't retraceable to the same source. The original narrative underwent some change, as so often happens in the retelling. It doesn't really matter. In fact, the variations on the same theme enrich it.

The talent Matthew refers to was the largest piece of currency, worth a hundred days' wage. It was a coin worth its weight in gold, silver or precious metal in Palestine and Syria. For Hebrews and Greeks it was, like pounds, a medium of exchange. Talent also refers to an individual's "native ability," his or her mental or physical aptitude for performing some specific task.

"Talent" is still current in common parlance. We speak of people engaged as talent scouts in sports and theater, of talent shows on radio and TV, and of talented young ladies who compete in beauty contests, where the winners are awarded an assortment of prizes.

For some unaccountable reason, the number three is featured in folk tales. So, three servants are left with their master's funds as in a trust, "each in proportion to his ability."

Is this master a merchant, the ancient counterpart of the

businessman or banker? Possibly, though the identity of the master or man of noble birth varies from the one gospel version to the other.

"Servants" is a standard metaphor for whom? Israel? The law-abiding Pharisees in the time of Jesus? Or religious leaders generally? Hard to say exactly who the servants represent. They're handed something similar to a trust fund, to be turned into capital gains. The trust may symbolize any kind of gift, even the first gift of life itself. Insofar as all of the servants have a native ability, they represent anyone of us.

The valuable talent which has to be put to work to prove fidelity to the master, isn't our own but a share "in the riches of Christ." His return—will it come early or late? Jesus suggests later, while the period in-between will be a time to test our use and development of the talents we've been given. By applying the moral to ourselves, and not simply to religious leaders or others, we have to examine our use of time, health, intelligence and above all, God's grace. Does it pay to incur the displeasure of Jesus by frittering away the eternal life we received at baptism?

The original trust fund contains other gifts as well: the emotions that enliven life, the powers of intelligence and free will, family life, friends. You name them. The riches for which we're accountable include all we have received from the dawn of reason to the twilight of life. The potential for growth in Christ is enormous.

The life-story of St. Paul exemplifies one who has concern and care for the treasures he has received, especially the gift of the Christian faith, which he has kept even in the face of hardship. "But I have not lost confidence, because I know who it is that I have put my trust in, and I have no doubt at all that he is able to take care of all that I have entrusted to him until that Day"—the Day of Judgment (2 Tm 1:12). The trust in question is sound Christian doctrine or apostolic good, kept intact. Together with his own concern is the care for his friend Timothy:

"My dear Timothy, take great care of all that has been entrusted to you"—everything belonging to the life of faith (1 Tm 6:20). "You have been trusted to look after something precious . . ." (2 Tm 1:14). Thanks to the fidelity and sincerity of Paul and his proteges preaching and teaching the word of God, the faith has been handed on like a deposit, safe and secure.

A contemporary retelling would probably have a rich investor hand his portfolio over to three brokers who manage parts of it while the "master" is abroad on business, vacationing, or sailing his yacht. The first of the brokers is a speculator in stocks, the riskiest venture, but if shrewd and lucky, he may receive the most return from his investment, doubling or tripling it in a short time. The second broker is interested in growth stock, which is a surer bet for him but still highly profitable. The third wants to play it safe; he hoards the securities. He has no spirit of enterprise, no entrepreneurship, as the other two have. Is he self-seeking? Or is he anticipating a promotion for his caution in a wild market? In any case, he accuses his client of greed. The client commends the first two for their fidelity, courage and activity, but charges the third with neglect of his duty, which was to gain interest, dividend or capital assets.

In rabbinic law, which the third broker apparently follows, burying one's wealth is the safest way to preserve it, like putting money into a safety deposit box or into a sock. The Lukan version has the servant rolling the pound into a piece of linen, which doesn't excuse the servant from liability if the money is lost. In short, the safe tactic pays off nothing for the broker.

The three servants eventually are rewarded or punished for their use or disuse of their innate abilities. Their reward is both this-worldly and other-worldly in the kingdom of heaven. The this-worldly accrues from greater responsibility, as the saying goes, "The reward of duty (done) is a duty (to be done)."

Luke, however, writes about a this-worldly punishment for the good-for-nothing servant. Even what he has is taken away from him and bestowed on the others, which raises the question of distributive justice. Is life unjust?

Frankly, the complaint about the distributive justice of God is unjust, for there's absolutely nothing in his kingdom to lay claim to. All is gift, all is grace. The variety of talents or pounds is never overburdening or overdemanding beyond the grace sufficient for us, never beyond our ability. The trust of this world's goods, well invested, well managed, wins an other-worldly reward.

12

A TIME FOR PLANTING, FOR UPROOTING

Mt 13:24-30, 36-43

Any amateur gardener of flowers and vegetables has experienced firsthand the contest between plants and weeds. They know that good garden care will assure that the weeds are the losers. Taking the easy way to a "victory garden," one may try for a time to prevent weeds with weed killer but remain worried by environmental reports that chemicals infest crops and kill wild life. With no weed killer at hand, the sower has no alternative but to allow the weeds to grow with the wheat till harvest season.

Picture a Palestinian wheat field, ripe, golden, waving in the breeze. Looking at it from afar, no darnel or tares appear in it, because in its early stages of growth darnel resembles wheat. The owner himself doesn't notice the darnel at first, having sowed good seed in his field. During the night an enemy of his played a dirty trick on him. The owner has to come to a quick decision in response to his servants' discovery and question. "Wait for the harvest," is his answer.

"What's the explanation of this comparison to the kingdom of heaven?" the disciples ask. The explanation on record probably is more Matthean than Jesus' own. The reason is that Matthew changes the point of the story, emphasizing the day of final judgment when the saintly will be separated from the sinful. Jesus has another point to make, which we will see.

47

Some contemporaries of his wonder why he doesn't clean up the world, get rid of the tax collectors and sinners, and associate only with the pure and holy. John the Baptizer had promised that the Messiah would bring about just such a separation. "His winnowing-fan is in his hand; he will clear his threshing floor and gather his wheat into the barn; but the chaff he will burn in a fire that will never go out" (Mt 3:12). A similar objection is raised later against Peter, the head of the new Church, for his hobnobbing with Gentiles.

The objection must have arisen out of the spirit of the times, for there were other messiahs and other groups in Israel whose goal was to achieve *pure* holiness, like gathering pure honey. The Essene community at Qumran had this goal in life. The Pharisees were named "the separated" because fearful of contamination, they held themselves aloof from sinners.

Now we know *why* Jesus responds with the parable of "the wheat and the darnel." We realize at once that they stand respectively for good and bad people who co-exist in the world and commingle in the Church. In order to let the darnel grow there's no insinuation of letting sin and crime continue or increase, without any efforts at reform and renewal. The owner wisely lets the two grow up together, seeing that it's too late in the season to uproot the darnel. Its roots are so intertwined with the wheat that only the harvest can separate them without damaging the wheat.

The young wheat and darnel are so alike that they're not that much different in their early stages. Because we can't always discern good and evil in their early stages either, we may let minor faults grow up into intractable bad habits. The saying goes that as the twig is bent so grows the tree. If only bad habits were eventually as eradicable as darnel!

The wheat farmer in fact harvests the darnel itself. How? In Israel, for lack of fuel, he has it tied into bundles like twigs and branches to be burnt. So, in a sense, he harvests a double crop, capitalizing on a crime.

His real enemy then isn't even the darnel but the hostile planter. Who is he but the devil, known earlier in sacred history by the name of Satan. Is it true that he's still public enemy #1, or has he been demythologized out of existence? If we acknowledge his existence as Jesus himself seemed to, then we should fear him as a source of evil, planting its seed into human life. The world and the flesh provide him with fields in which to sow. Our human life is bedeviled when the desires of the flesh and of the eyes and the pride of life are given into. Darnel symbolizes every kind of worldly evil that disguises itself as good and, once it sinks its roots deep into our lives, isn't easily uprooted.

The fire which finally consumes the darnel is the punishing fire of Gehenna which forever burns away every defilement. Once belief in the devil disappears, it seems consistent that belief in hell should go with it, that is, eternal punishment or everlasting separation from God. On the other hand, it seems to follow that those who separate themselves from God in the present life be disassociated from him in eternal life.

We're back to the problem of association or company-keeping. Did Jesus intend his Church to be without sinners, as a field without darnel? Paul in his letter to the Ephesians says of Christ and his Church: "He made her clean by washing her in water with a form of words [baptism], so that when he took her to himself she would be glorious, with no speck or wrinkle or anything like that, but holy and faultless" (Ep 5:26-27). That's an ideal picture of the Church at the end-time, but in the meanwhile "the Church is a tract of land to be cultivated, the field of God," where plants and weeds are likely to grow up together (1 Cor 3:9; cf. *Lumen Gentium* #6). Is it even possible for the Church to keep company only with the holy? No. Throughout her history she's not been without "the human failings of those to whom the gospel is entrusted," and she ceaselessly exhorts her people "to purify and renew [themselves] so that the sign of Christ can shine more brightly on the face of the Church" (*Gaudium et Spes*, #43).

God still draws good out of evil, and always allows the possibility and opportunity for sinners to repent. The Church of Christ rejects premature separation and recommends patience till the harvest season. With our common human failings to cope with, our personal mixture of good and evil, we in the Church can't see clearly enough to separate wheat from darnel. We are too prone to errors of judgment. The Church will be fully revealed, pure and holy in God's sight and by his means, only at the last.

13

THE PEARL OF A TREASURE

Mt 13:44-46

True to their nature, "the treasure" and "the pearl" read like twin folk tales. Jesus often recalled folk tales. That's one reason why he was so popular. But he didn't simply repeat them. He surprised his listeners with new twists to the old and familiar.

Buried in his stories like a treasure or a pearl is wisdom. "[In ancient wisdom] if you look for it [wisdom] as if it were silver, and search for it as for buried treasure, you will understand what the fear of Yahweh is, and discover the knowledge of God" (Pr 2:4-5). Yet seeking the wisdom of God is unlike searching for a lost coin along a street or path, or unlike using a metal detector which beeps over a precious piece of metal. "The beginning of wisdom? The acquisition of wisdom; at the cost of all you have, acquire perception" (Pr 4:7). Its acquisition must be worth the effort.

Hidden treasure was a folk motif in the ancient Near East. Rich Palestinians used to cache their valuables underground during the invasions and wars which they had to suffer from two sides, Mesopotamia and Egypt. The two powers kept Palestine in an almost perpetual state of siege. The cache remained buried until its discovery.

In the element of such a surprise discovery, "the treasure"

51

and "the pearl" are like fraternal twins resembling each other and yet showing dissimilarities, born like Jacob and Esau. They differ as much as the poor and the rich, the have-nots and the haves. The kingdom they symbolize means as much to the farmhand as to the merchant. With their discovery, the one and the other can rise above their past status.

The farmhand came upon the hidden treasure by chance, a stroke of good luck. He unearthed a jar containing silver coins or perhaps jewels left behind by a wealthy landowner who had to flee for his life. The farmhand kept the secret of his find and reburied it, a procedure which in rabbinic law was a security against theft. As a poor man, he had to sell all his property to buy the field, although he was happy over getting a bargain.

The rich merchant, on the contrary, had to seek and find fine pearls. Pearls were valued as a great prize in antiquity, sought and found in the Red Sea, Persian Gulf and Indian Ocean. They were worn as ornaments, worth millions, especially as necklaces. Cleopatra, the Egyptian queen, wore a particularly expensive pearl necklace.

The phrase, "sell everything," is challenging, suggesting a willingness to sacrifice everything for the sake of the kingdom of heaven. The kingdom does lay down an imperative—the will of God. But an overemphasis on the sacrifice may discourage them who seek the kingdom. As a matter of fact, there's no sacrifice, or it's minimal, in giving up property in exchange for a value incomparably greater. Everything else is remote and secondary to the great joy which the farmhand and merchant feel in discovering treasure and pearl. Everything else pales in comparison. The discoverers are only too happy to pay the price of their new discovery. Likewise the true disciple seeking the kingdom of heaven and finding it, experiences an overwhelming joy.

A novel in American literature titled *The Pearl*, written by John Steinbeck, has some of the same elements as the two folk tales. Originally his was a true story; Steinbeck presented it as folk-lore.

In his narrative the pearl fisherman or diver is a young man, Kino, who goes out daily in his canoe, his prize possession, and dives for pearls lying at the bottom of the sea. He has to weigh himself down with a rock tied about his waist. He meets with danger at sea, a life-threatening occupational hazard. But he's motivated by love for his wife Juana and their only child Coyotito. He yearns for the day when he will discover a really big, giant pearl, the sale of which will supply his wife with the clothes, the food, the house he wants for her and an education for their child.

Eventually Kino comes up with an oyster shell containing "the great pearl, perfect as the moon. It was as large as a sea gull's egg. It was the greatest pearl in the world." The news of Kino's great discovery, "The Pearl of the World," spread throughout his hometown.

Then the troubles begin for Kino and his family.

The local priest tries to figure out how much the sale of the pearl will bring for payment of repairs to the church. Shopkeepers anticipate big sales in the future. The doctor who earlier refused treatment to Kino and Juana's child because they were unable to pay for it, claims him as a patient and dreams about a luxurious vacation in Paris. Even the beggars in front of the church see an opportunity ahead for themselves, for they know how generous a poor man is with his sudden wealth.

The men most excited over Kino's discovery are the little traders who buy pearls from the fishermen. They cackle, fight, shout, threaten for the cheapest buy they can get. They know when to stop their hard bargaining lest the fisherman donate the pearl to the church. The semblance of competition among them drives up the cost of the pearl, but in reality there's just one capitalist, their employer, who keeps up the charade. The buyers wait and hope for the day they can succeed their boss and take his place.

At first Kino and his wife Juana don't see this dark, treacherous side of life because they're so exicted and happy over the Pearl of the World. They believe everyone shares their joy.

They see in the pearl visions of the future, of the things they planned having in the past but had to forego. In short order, though, they come to realize evil has befallen them: there are attempts at stealing the pearl, attempts on the life of Kino, Juana and the child. Juana cries, "This thing is evil. This pearl is like a sin! It will destroy us. Throw it away Kino. . . ." She tries to steal out of their shack and throw the pearl away, but he catches her in the act.

When pearl merchants refuse to pay Kino the true value of the pearl, he and his wife leave town stealthily, thinking they can deal better elsewhere. In the course of their escape the life of Coyotito is lost through a murderous assault on the family.

Juana, carrying the dead child in her arms, and Kino return to their hometown. Together they go out to sea. They throw the Pearl of the World into the water and watch it sink to the bottom, buried.

We are left with the wisdom of a choice between the kingdom of heaven as the treasure or the Pearl of the World.

14

LIKE FATHER, LIKE SON

Mt 20:1-16

Is it possible that in the vineyard of the Lord—Israel or the Church—the vintage is "sour grapes," a cry from victims of injustice? What is the vintage to be, from first to last?

The story of the vineyard took on special meaning for me thanks to three experiences I had with vineyards and grape-culture. The first goes back many years to a pilgrimage to Fatima. The Italian liner stopped for a day at Lisbon, allowing its passengers to disembark and take an excursion bus ride to Fatima. We drove through hilly and stony countryside where olives and grapes grew on terraced ground. It was late summer when the grape harvest was ready. Along the way the harvesters were returning with grape-loaded carts. The aroma of grapes— already fermenting, much to my surprise—filled the air. The whole scene left not only a pleasant memory but that sense of urgency the harvesters must have felt. If delayed, the grape harvest would have lost much of its value. No wonder the landowner in the gospel story was glad to have the workers at hand to hire.

Then there was the experience of picking grapes in Mary-land. They, too, were fully ripe and had to be picked carefully on a hot, humid morning. This wasn't however, "a heavy day's work

55

in all the heat," for the grapes were homegrown on a small arbor and picked at the invitation of the owner. The harvest was sufficient for making several gallons of homemade wine to be shared—a surprise gift—with friends and benefactors.

The next experience was a tour of a vineyard in the southwestern corner of Wisconsin. The vineyard was situated on a hillside facing west. The first attempt of the landowner, an immigrant, met with failure because he didn't reckon with the severe Wisconsin winters. A tree standing alongside a window of the main building, nourished by the mash tossed out to it, survived to be 175 years old! Later, hardier grapevines were developed, and other owners saw the vineyard grow into a fair business and tourist attraction.

To whom did Jesus first proclaim the message of the vineyard? To his disciples? To the Scribes and Pharisees who had been protesting against him? The one thing we know for sure is that it's addressed to us, and we're inclined to take it on our own terms.

One of our first impressions is that it deals with fair labor practices and distributive justice. But this seems to deflect us momentarily from its original meaning.

There's the matter of the work schedule. The landowner summons workers in five shifts, from daybreak to about 5:00 p.m. The first shift works about 12 hours, the last only an hour. The working conditions aren't the same for all workers. Some have to sweat through the heat of the day. The sun's heat explains why it's urgent to gather the harvest—the grapes are ripening fast, all the sweeter for the sunshine. The landowner is pressed for time, even more than the workers, as he runs the risk of losing a prime harvest.

Unemployment is also a factor in the case. The landowner isn't about to let capable and willing workers stand idle. A high rate of unemployment is harmful to any society. Economic depression or recession keep people poor, but more distressing yet is that they diminish human dignity. By hiring the idle the landowner does them a favor and draws profit for himself from a good harvest.

He promises to pay the first crew a fair wage. The denarius is a just daily wage, enough for a livelihood, but no more. The wage, however, causes the first crew to grumble. The last to be paid see what the latecomers are getting and complain in the name of distributive justice. The landowner defends himself on the score that he hasn't promised a *quid pro quo* payment. In another work situation the laborers would have had cause for complaint. But that's beside the point here.

What then is the real issue? It seems to be something more pertinent than justice.

What if the landowner is God? What if the vineyard is the world? What if the workers include all of us, all humanity, both early and latecomers? Both Jews and Gentiles? Both the faithful and social outcasts? As he does repeatedly, Jesus suggests a sense of urgency: We aren't allowed all the time in the world to set affairs straight before the coming of his kingdom. Along the way to entrance there's no place or time for idlers. The human harvest is ripe. We have to prove ourselves equal to a lifetime task.

The overriding question Jesus asks is: "What is God like?" The picture emerging from the story is that of Someone Who is all-good, full of generosity: "I am generous." He's large-hearted, with a heart of goodness and compassion for the poor, the unemployed and their families. God is the Great Benefactor of humanity, the Perfect Philanthropist, giving 100%-plus. His gift-giving is wrapped in pleasant *surprises*. If justice enters at all into this tale of generosity, it's in contrast to God's bountiful goodness.

In his kingdom everything is *gift*, nothing is *wage*. The nature of a gift contradicts something bargained or contracted for. When God asks us to labor in his kingdom, the initiative is

his, and we really have no claim to a fair wage, primarily or
fundamentally. We must say to ourselves, "We are merely
servants: we have done no more than our duty" (Lk 17:10).

The picture of God Who is all-good and generous, the
Giver of life in his kingdom, serves as a backdrop to the life of
Jesus himself. What is the spirit of his own life, message and
work if not that of generosity? Jesus the storyteller is implying of
himself: "I act the same way as my Father. I defend my own
action of befriending all races and classes of people. The common denominator in my treatment of all people is goodness.
Have I no right to do what I like with my own? Why be envious
because I am generous?" The vineyard of the world, thick and
heavy with vines and grapes, bears a good harvest for all
humanity.

The overwhelming goodness of God imaged in Jesus still
has the element of surprise: What is there left of his goodness to
see?

15

A Pretty Kettle of Fish

Mt 13:47-50

We boys used to fish off the concrete bridge in Stange Park,
which hangs over the Prairie River from the park to the public
library. The river had what we called "stonerollers" or "suckers"
swimming in it. Despite their unappetizing names, they were
edible fish, especially if caught in the early spring water. On a
clear day, they could be spotted from the bridge, floating lazily
after breakfast among the rocks. We fished them out with a
three-pronged hook, without bait. All we had to do was pull the
hook in front of them, carefully, and then jerk it at them.

I was fishing off the bridge when a gang of older and bigger
boys came along and, pretending to show me how to fish, they
took over the line and were catching fish of all sizes. After they
loaded me down with two strings of fish, large and small, I had
no more heart for fishing. I took the fish home, but my mother
saw there were too many for us to eat, and some were too small
to bother about, so I had to clean some and throw the rest away.

The lesson of the fishnet is the same. It hauls in both good
and bad fish. Actually, its point of view shifts from the separation of fish to the kingdom of heaven. The pedagogical method
of Jesus is two-pronged: living and effective, judging and
dividing.

In his ministry to Israel, Jesus makes no excuse for the fact that his disciples are a motley group. They will have their ranks thinned out by a process of elimination at the end-time. His company till the final judgment is to be a gathering-in of all kinds of people.

The invitation he extends to fishermen reads, "Follow me and I will make you fishers of men" (Mt 4:19). Somehow the setting fits the Sea of Galilee or Gennesareth, where much fishing takes place. The sea, like the mountain, is more than a geographical place in the life story of Jesus. It provides a religious backdrop full of theological symbolism—it *reveals*. Twenty-four species of fish have been counted in this "sea-kettle." Ancient peoples thought 153 varieties of fish existed in all. From this number, a symbol of all the nations of the world, we catch some idea of the races of people that swim in the sea of life, and the universal-sized net of Jesus.

Fish-netting requires special skill. The fishnet (dragnet or seine-net) is either pulled between two boats, or behind or alongside a single boat. A fishnet can't be selective of fish as can a bait or trap or lure. Fishermen who go net-fishing or turn into fishers of men, have to take what they get. Only later can they toss out the undesirable catch. In olden days no fishing licenses were issued to limit the size and number of fish that could be caught.

The only rule fishermen went by was laid down in the Book of Leviticus: "Of all that lives in water, these you may eat. . . . Anything that lives in water, but has no fins or scales, is to be held detestable" (11:9-12). This rule differentiated the good from the bad fish, the edible from the inedible. The inedible or unclean fish were snake-like or crabs. The criterion for the selection of fish or any other food was cleanliness. Clean food was edible and worthy to be offered to God at worship. Cleanliness, in other words, was next to Godliness.

But while fishermen were in the business of netting fish,

they had no time to sort them out. The sorting-out had to wait till the end of the fishing trip. The fishnet therefore has a meaning for the future of human life, an eschatological cast. The separation of humans, good and bad, must wait till the final judgment, the end-time.

No one knows for sure the date of its coming. "There must be no passing of premature judgment," says St. Paul in 1 Cor 4:5. The reason for postponing judgment can readily be surmised. We humans are unable to judge effectively or exactly, for we can judge only externals, not the motives of the human heart. We frequently err. Faith and patience in human trials dictate that we leave judgment to the Lord.

A more cogent reason for relinquishing judgment to him is that it belongs to him by right. He has set the time for it. Already in his lifetime, he was urged to clean house. Separatist groups were gathering already then, but Jesus shied away from them. He didn't intend to establish a pure, holy, righteous, just, spiritual elite. Nor was he about to be conclusively selective or judgmental before the fullness of time.

The fishnet, the gathering-in of good and bad fish, is a metaphor which holds true of the Church of Christ as well as of the kingdom of heaven. Just as Jesus "has come to seek out and save what was lost" (Lk 19:10), "similarly, the Church [which is part of the kingdom and purposes to bring about the kingdom] encompasses with love all those who are afflicted with human weakness." Vatican II stated in its Dogmatic Constitution on the Church, "the Church, embracing sinners in her bosom, is at the same time holy and always in need of being purified, and incessantly pursues the path of penance and renewal" (#8).

We read in the Decree on Ecumenism the same confession of the Church of sinners: "Christ summons the Church, as she goes her pilgrim way, to that continual reformation of which she always has need, insofar as she is an institution of men here on earth" (#6). Deficiencies do occur in her doctrine, discipline, and deportment, like tears in a fishnet.

The only judgment allowable in the Church before the final judgment and the separation at the end-time will necessarily be a negative one: "If we say that we have not sinned, we make him [Christ] a liar, and his word is not in us" (1 Jn 1:10). The Decree on Ecumenism adds the comment: "This holds good for sins against unity" (#7).

If anyone but God selected and judged, we would have a pretty kettle of fish for consumption.

16

A Friendly Intruder

Lk 11:5-8

Jesus would have us contemplate a scene, put ourselves into a real-life situation where we receive a midnight call from an unexpected guest.

The gospel writer Luke sees the situation as the context for an instruction on *how* to pray and get results.

To construct the scene: the guest arrives at a one-room house in an Oriental village. The time is night when the villager and his family have long been to bed according to the native custom of retiring early. The entire family sleeps together in the room, lying on the floor mat. It is a poor family by our standard of living. The house is dark but for a small oil lamp burning faintly. The door, bolted with an iron or wooden bar thrust through rings, would, upon unbolting, make noise enough to awaken the whole family.

There's a knock at the door, a neighbor has just received a visit from a friend and, in a spirit of Oriental hospitality, wants to offer a welcome tray but has no bread. He asks the householder for a normal portion, three loaves, because in their clustered conditions the Palestinian villagers know who has bread left over. His intention is to borrow the bread and replenish it in the morning, the Palestinian practice being to bake bread before dawn.

We're to imagine ourselves primarily in the role of the protagonist, the sleepy-eyed friend, not as the petitioner. If we unbolt the door, the commotion will rouse the entire family. But if we send the friend away empty-handed, we betray a friendship. We feel ourselves caught in a dilemma, put to a test of friendship.

The heavy, urgent knock at the door is symbolic of a cry for help. In the Lukan gospel it expresses a prayer: ". . . Knock, and the door will be opened to you . . . The one who knocks will always have the door opened to him" (11:10).

Is there something special in the fact that the knock is for bread? Bread comprises all human needs whatever, as in the Our Father: "Give us this day our daily bread." Do we value this "bread" enough to ask for it in daily prayer? St. Ambrose celebrated Mass every day, and St. Monica, a devoted friend of his, habitually attended this Mass. One of his sermons contrasts manna with the Bread of Life which is available daily. It compares, too, the abundance of the heavenly banquet with the hardship of harvesting food and drink from the earth, the annual produce with the daily provision of the Eucharistic Christ, spiritual food and drink.

Shuffling to the door as a sleepy-eyed friendly neighbor, what would motivate us to open the door and accede to the want of the caller? Possibly two things.

"For friendship's sake." For a reflection on this motive, there's scarcely anything better than the philosophical oration of Cicero on friendship. He has an important and wise contribution to make from his own religious beliefs and philosophy of life. His high-minded thought lays down as the first law of friendship "that we should ask from friends, and do for friends, only what is good." Remember the old saying, "A friend in need is a friend indeed"? We shouldn't wait to be asked but be ever ready and unhesitant to help a friend. For this bit of the philosophy of friendship the Roman Cicero is dependent on the wisdom of the Greeks, just as the Hebrews of the Old Testament drew some of their wisdom from the same source.

The quality to look for in a friend—to see whether his friendship isn't a mere casual acquaintanceship but something stable and permanent—is loyalty. It's to be found in a friend who is simple, social-minded, sympathetic. Cicero is suspicious of characters who are complex and deceitful. They give the impression of not knowing which political way to turn; they may leave us standing at the door, knocking.

Good and wise friendship, Cicero asserts, allows for no make-believe, no pretense. It's open and above-board, pleasant-mannered and good natured. Endowed with such qualities, friends prevent accusations, criticisms and suspicions.

As families in the same Palestinian village come to know one another only gradually, so friendship takes time to grow and prosper. An old proverb Cicero quotes sets great store by the test of time: "You must eat many a peck of salt with a man to be thorough friends with him."

The other motive for helping out a friend is the nobler of the two: faith. Assuming the householder to be God, Luke unhesitatingly honors this theological motive and its human counterpart, trust. He encourages prayer, to make our requests known to God even at a time supposedly inconvenient to him. Why not, if God "the guardian of Israel does not doze or sleep" (Ps 121:4)? "Whatever you ask for in my name I will do," Jesus promised, "so that the Father may be glorified in the Son. If you ask anything in my name, I will do it" (Jn 14:13-14). The "Open, Sesame!" to God is the name of the Son.

It's inconceivable that God should turn us away from the door of his household in the middle of the night. Has he anything but heavenly hospitality?

The answer to the prayer of petition depends not nearly as much on how steady and persistent it is as on the certainty that

God won't fail to answer. He responds readily to the cry of the needy who are confident of his promise of help.

Petitionary prayer must have a heavy, urgent knock, nonetheless. The combination to the door of heaven is an unwavering trust. God supplies the wonder bread for our daily needs.

The friendly intruder awakens us to the need of daily prayer. Trust in friendship, trust in a Friend.

17

A BROTHER'S KEEPER

Lk 10:25-37

On the 16-mile highway trip to the city, a total stranger lies injured, practically lifeless. Would we pull up alongside, bandage him up, and rush him to the emergency room at the nearest hospital? And if he had no insurance policy or Medicare, would we be willing to pay for his hospitalization? A rather large order, granted, yet not too far-fetched from the situation the Good Samaritan found himself in as he traveled by ox or donkey the 17-mile stretch from Jerusalem to Jericho.

Before the assault, was the stranger aware of the danger of robbery threatening along that route? Perhaps he tried to defend himself and in the act of self-defense was beaten within an inch of his life. The Samaritan made medicinal use of oil and wine. He "soothed with oil" (Is 1:6) and disinfected the man's wounds with wine. He set him on his beast of burden and took him to a nearby inn. Most likely, the Samaritan was a merchant who frequented the inn, so the innkeeper took the payment of a day's board (1/12 of a denarius) and trusted the Samaritan to pay the balance later.

Popular stories such as this usually had three principal characters in them. Example: a priest, a levite, and a Samaritan. Without the other two characters, the story loses its bite; it fails to disturb the conscience.

It raises once again the disturbing problem of religion, race and social relations. Did Jesus know about the trick the Samaritans played on the Palestinians several years before? That they littered the courtyard of the Jerusalem temple with dead men's bones during the Passover season?

The touch of a corpse spread uncleanness. The Book of Leviticus forbade priests and levites (associates of priests) from approaching the corpse of relatives, unless it was that of a father, mother, son, daughter or brother. It was forbidden to touch even the corpse of an unmarried sister; by marriage she lost all blood ties.

Leviticus 21:1-3 may explain why the priest and levite passed by the robbery victim. They may have thought he was dead, and even for mercy's sake weren't about to disobey the law. In the conduct of their worship, the religious officials and leaders of Israel had to keep themselves neat and tidy.

The third character to appear should have been a Jewish layman, which would have brought the anti-clerical feeling to the fore. Instead, Jesus introduced a Samaritan layman. Why? Because he belonged to a mixed race, a minority group. His family had been Israelite, but inter-married with foreign colonists. By inter-marriage he was neither full Jew nor full Gentile. Jews and Samaritans engaged in a long, non-speaking rivalry. Samaritans, having been refused worship at the Jerusalem temple, had their own temple and version of the Pentateuch.

The robbery victim is left anonymous; he's simply a "neighbor." Does "neighbor" have to be the same race: Jew, black, native American; or of the same religion: Roman Catholic, Protestant, Jewish, Moslem?

Because sidestepping the above question is ethically inexcusable, Jesus switches the question around. Rather than inquire about who the *object* of compassion, love, or mercy is, he asks for proof of neighborliness, that is, for the *subject* of love and mercy. Who then is the real neighbor?

The answer emerges from the biblical teaching on the primacy of love. Deuteronomy 6:5 reads: "You shall love Yahweh your God with all your heart, with all your soul, with all your strength." If the whole self is involved in the love of God, is there any love left for anybody else? Paradoxically, the commandment of love is doubled: "You must love your neighbor as yourself" (Lv 19:18). In either case, God or neighbor, love remains the same, of equal weight. The resolution of the question lies in love unlimited. The opportunity for love and mercy extends to everybody, hence the robbery victim is everybody in need of love.

The Good Samaritan plot revolves around the Jewish dislike of the Samaritans. Early in the gospel of John, when Jesus reveals himself to the Samaritan woman at Jacob's well, she exclaims, "What? You are a Jew and you ask me, a Samaritan, for a drink?" (4:9). John comments: "Jews, in fact, do not associate with Samaritans." Later in the same gospel, when the Jews tangle with Jesus over his claim to relationship to God the Father, they accuse him: "Are we not right in saying that you are a Samaritan and possessed by a devil?" (8:48). Jesus a Samaritan? He does befriend the marginalized in religion and society, the poor, ignorant and immigrant. On the one hand, he's suspect for his association with Samaritans; on the other, he's accused of being a Samaritan himself.

God *and* neighbor that he is, Jesus doesn't act contrary to his gospel, for mercy or compassion is central to it. What's more, the supreme evangelical challenge to Jew and Gentile alike is to be "compassionate as (the) Father is compassionate," to be "kind to the ungrateful and the wicked" (Lk 6:35-36). In the gospel context, the Good Samaritan appears as a Christ-figure.

St. Thomas Aquinas in his theological treatise on the virtue of love considers its interior effects, one of which is mercy (the other two are joy and peace). For his analysis of mercy he depends much on the philosopher Aristotle and quotes him: "We pity most the distress of one who suffers undeservedly"— the robbery victim, for example.

To the question, "To whom does it belong to pity?" Thomas replies that the one who pities regards another's distress as his own. "For, since he who loves another looks upon his friend as another self, he counts his friend's hurt as his own, so that he grieves for his friend's hurt as though he were hurt himself. Hence the philosopher . . . reckons grieving with one's friend as being one of the signs of friendship. . . ."

Pity for the distressed grows the more we realize that the same distress may one day befall us. "This also explains," Thomas continues, "why the old and wise who consider that they may fall upon evil times, as also feeble and timorous persons, are more inclined to pity. . . ."

The Good Samaritan was wise. Was he also old, feeble or timorous?

18

TEARS OF PENANCE

Lk 7:36-50

The debt that hangs over the heads of two debtors is like a penance that is overdue. Since Luke is the only evangelist to hand down their story, it's really a defense of the entire gospel of Jesus and his preaching of penance. This is how Luke sees Jesus.

Jesus' earthly task, as was his predecessor John the Baptist's, is to preach penance. Eventually Jesus makes it clear that he's to pour out his blood for sinners. And, in time, his followers, too, come to realize that he was put to death in atonement for their sins and not for some revolutionary or political cause (Rm 4:25). Jesus is sent to bring good news to the poor (Lk 4:18) and is recognized as "a friend of . . . sinners" (Lk 7:34).

The larger context—the wide-angle camera shot—turns upon the two debtors, and then the camera's eye focuses on Simon the Pharisee's house, where Jesus has been invited to a meal, possibly to more than a simple meal, for other guests are present, and even outsiders may join in the conversation. In due course the question arises, "Who is this man, that he even forgives sins?" Appropriately this meal, like the Eucharist itself, is an occasion for reconciliation.

Luke protects the good name of the woman even though she has a reputation for loose morals. She waits upon Jesus, head

71

and foot. She doesn't spare herself. Her tears, flowing over his feet, symbolize washing, a mark of hospitality and courtesy to one who has to travel by foot. Then, shame doesn't keep her from loosening her hair in public, and wiping his feet with her hair and kissing them. By anointing his head she confers on him her respect and honor. Distracted all the while by her reputation, Simon extends none of these courtesies. Jesus reads his thoughts and responds to them.

He intimates that the creditor is God. God's goodness, actually his unmitigated mercy, is manifest. Debt is the equivalent of guilt. God is willing to cancel out all guilt, great and small. In return he expects a proportionate show of gratitude. For much that has been forgiven, much thankful love is due, like the tears of this poor woman. The Pharisee, when Jesus asks him which of the debtors is the more grateful, answers correctly. St. Ambrose comments on his reply: "The Pharisee's judgment is praised, but his affection is disapproved."

St. Ambrose sent a fairly long letter to his sister Marcellina interpreting this Lukan passage, and makes an application of it to his own time. His letters to his sister generally reflect the then current history. There was an ongoing struggle between the synagogue and the Church, and Ambrose defended the Church against the synagogue, just as Jesus took the part of the repentant woman against Simon the Pharisee.

Ambrose says that Christians in the Church experience both "the water of baptism" and "the tears of penance." Truly, the water of baptism—immersing Christians in the death and resurrection of Jesus—washes away all sin, original and personal. There was a tendency in the early Church to postpone baptism till the moment of death, because the sacrament of penance may not have been as available then as it is now.

Ambrose contends that the tears of penance, along with the forgiveness of sin, is a gift greater than baptism. "If he (God) had forgiven only our first debts, he would have seemed more cautious than generous, more intent on our correction than magnanimous . . . He first bestows . . . a gift in baptism, and later He is most generous with His gifts . . . He saw us bound by a heavy debt. No one could pay his debt with his inheritance of innocence. . . ."

In the table conversation at the Pharisee's house, we overhear, as it were, the correct attitude *toward* sinners, and at the same time the grateful attitude *of* the sinner.

The Church, hardly any more today than in her past, confesses the fact of sin and upholds penance. At Vatican II, she admitted to taking sinners to her bosom. And in her search for truth she also found that certitude, in consequence of sin, was always "partly obscured and weakened." The Church today seeks answers to the "mysteries of the human condition," and specifically to the question, "What is sin?" Affected by original sin, all peoples fall into error. Whether or not the world is worse off today than ever before in the history of humankind isn't easy to discern. Still, the fact of the matter is that there has been an enormous multiplication of sin.

Since Vatican II, a series of documents have been issued by Rome on the value of penance. The Apostolic Constitution on Penance by Paul VI, in 1966, took note of the value in the Church of little acts of penance: "Every suffering and sorrow" is joined to the cross of Christ and subsumed into the sacramental satisfaction or penance. In this age of comfort, all discomforts are means of penance, provided they're accepted with the right interior attitude.

As Ambrose perceived the "tears of penance" flowing with the "water of baptism," so the Church in her 1970 Decree on Confession for Religious, encouraged the frequent use of the sacrament of penance. The decree stated that Jesus "restores and strengthens in the members of the Church who have sinned the fundamental gift of 'metanoia,' of conversion to the kingdom of Christ, which is first received in Baptism."

Beneficial too in the sacrament of penance is "a practice which (1) increases true knowledge of one's self, (2) favors Christian humility and (3) offers the occasion for salutary spiritual direction and (4) the increase of grace."

The new order of penance, the revision of the sacrament of penance was published in 1974. It provided for the private and communal celebration of the sacrament. It inculcated a spirit, an attitude Jesus recommended in the person of the repentant woman. It was *the* point of his conversation, and it's followed in the word of the confessor inviting all penitents to give thanks and to profess God's mercy: "Give thanks to the Lord, for he is good. For his mercy endures forever."

19

RICH MAN, POOR MAN

Lk 12:16-21

Flannery O'Connor, the southern Catholic novelist and short story writer, titled one of her short stories—the last before her death on August 3, 1964—"Judgment Day." It was published posthumously.

A poor white man, Tanner by name, shares a shack with a Negro servant in Corinth, Georgia. The servant has been with him for 30 years. Tanner feels a bond of friendship with Coleman, whose name puns on his blackness.

Tanner is visited by his daughter, married and living with her husband in the big city of New York. She prevails on her father in his late years to come and live comfortably with them in an apartment house. He grows very dissatisfied in New York. The air there he thinks is "the kind fit for cats and garbage." His sole aim is to return home, dead or alive. Homecoming is what matters to him—dead or alive doesn't. He has a strong sense of homecoming and a preoccupation with his place of burial. His attitude reflects an ancient, universal concern that the earthly resting place prefigures one's heavenly mansion. He holds his daughter to the promise to bury him in Corinth, or else she will "burn in hell."

The daughter who doesn't believe in hell, calls it "hardshell

Baptist hooey." Her concern is to have her father live "like decent people." The cantakerous old fellow wouldn't trade his shack for a million dollars. She thinks he should quit looking out the apartment window, pull up a chair to the TV, and "quit thinking about morbid stuff, death and hell and judgment. . . ."

Frustrated, he has a stroke, and while recovering from it dreams of getting shipped home in a pine box, and upon arrival he springs out of it, shouting to Coleman and a fellow Negro, "Judgment Day! Judgment Day! Don't you two fools know it's Judgment Day?"

Tanner dies, his daughter buries him in New York City, but she has such sleepless nights afterward, turning and tossing, that she has him dug up and hauled to Corinth. Only then does she rest well.

This modern setting and life situation match that of the rich man. In answer to the complaint of a man who desires part of an inheritance, Jesus cautions against avarice and security in riches.

The case of the gentleman farmer raises the question of the human attitude toward possessions: Does life consist in them? The rich landowner enjoys prosperity, yet seeks it all the more and looks forward to retirement in safe and complete ease and enjoyment: "to eat, drink and have a good time." But then sudden death befalls him; he has to leave his wealth behind. His property and goods are no investment in the kingdom to come.

The Old and New Testament differ in their attitudes toward wealth. The prospect of the future for people living in the Old Testament is prosperity in this life: "Wisdom builds a house with riches of every kind, rare and desirable" (Pr 24:4). But the same wisdom dictates distrust of wealth. Solomon, before getting rich, thinks: "I hold riches as nothing" (Ws 7:8-11). Wisdom is preferable to wealth. The wise man says, "He who trusts in riches will have his fall, the virtuous will flourish like the leaves" (Pr 11:28).

The reason why wisdom deems it folly to trust in riches, piling them up as if there were no tomorrow, is that riches blind their owners to the existence of God. "The fool says in his heart, 'There is no God' " (Ps 14:1). The wicked may think they will receive no punishment for evil, because "God forgets, he hides his face, he does not see at all" (Ps 10:4). That is why the farmer in the parable is called a fool.

Is there less of a warning against avarice or greed or death here—God does at times bestow wealth as a blessing—than a cry of impending doom, a harsh judgment? Repentance is urgent. Life is but a loan, time is borrowed, and an account of the stewardship of creation must be given.

Jesus announces judgment. At the parousia he will appear as judge. His final judgment will inaugurate the powerful and glorious reign of God. The end will bring a human harvest, not the distribution of a hoard.

Jesus prepares the world for judgment by the inevitability and severity of his death on the cross. His crucifixion is an occasion of judgment upon the world. The cross is his judgment seat, anticipating the final judgment. As the cross bears the burden of sin, so will the final judgment reveal the secrets of the heart, human attitudes toward God.

Surrounded by plentiful natural resources and wealth, we tend to forget divine sovereignty. God will come with power at the final judgment. The fool will discover that God is alive and well.

Jesus accentuates the truth that only in God is there real lasting wealth. He leaves this earthly life behind with absolutely nothing of his own, yet like a rich harvester he has a kingdom of heaven in store. The judgment of evil condemns him to the cross; the judgment of good bestows on him the reward of the eternal kingdom.

Further, Jesus teaches the straight-forward truth about "how hard it is for those who have riches to make their way into

the kingdom of God" (Lk 18:24). They're too heavily burdened
to travel there, too distracted by the goods of this world, and too
self-assured.

The old man, Tanner, fears no judgment because he has
acquired no wealth. And, humanly speaking, he wouldn't exchange his life and companionship with the black man, Coleman, for a million dollars.

Rich and poor, city-dweller and southerner, farmer and
fashionable society, all who live in and subscribe to the American
capitalistic system, are served a warning that they will never have
enough of earthly goods as security for the afterlife. Nor do
investments, insurance policies, and social security in life provide against the final judgment.

20

To Move Mountains

Mk 4:30-32;   Mt 13:31-32;   Lk 13:18-19

The "mustard seed," small as it is, appears only once in the liturgical Sunday readings. On the 11th Sunday, B Cycle, I brought a mustard seed to the lectern and during the homily exhibited it between my thumb and forefinger. The children strained to see it. Actually, none of them saw it at a distance, so after Mass some of them came up to see it close-at-hand. They marveled at it, as if I had plucked it out of the Bible.

The metaphor of the mustard seed tastes authentic, coming from Jesus without later editorializing. It's a Palestinian product, grown near Lake Gennesareth, proverbially the smallest of seeds, but not in reality. Nor is it a tree. It grows into a tall shrub, standing 8-10-12 feet high. Nor do the birds nest in it; they seek its shade for rest and its seeds for food. How the mustard seed grows into so tall a plant is a mystery of nature, and a hyperbole Jesus employs to sharpen its contrast of smallness with the greatness of the kingdom of God.

Jesus seems to have borrowed its imagery from the Old Testament account of how trees looked to the prophets. Ezekiel explains how trees are stunted and how they grow. "And every tree of the field will learn that I, Yahweh, am the one who stunts tall trees and makes the low ones grow, who withers green trees

79

and makes the withered green. I, Yahweh, have spoken, and I will do it" (17:24). Secretly and slowly Yahweh will supply the trees with inner strength and outer energy.

"From the top of the cedar, from the highest branch I will take a shoot and plant it myself on a very high mountain. I will plant it on the high mountain of Israel. It will sprout branches and bear fruit, and become a noble cedar. Every kind of bird will live beneath it" (Ezk 17:22-23; cf. 31:1-18).

King Nebuchadnezzar has a dream in which he sees a tree "with the birds of heaven nesting in its branches," which the prophet Daniel interprets for him: "The tree you saw that grew so tall and strong that it reached the sky and could be seen from the ends of the earth, the tree with beautiful foliage and abundant fruit, with food for all in it, providing shade for the wild animals, with the birds of heaven nesting in its branches, that tree is yourself, O king" (4:17-19). For the prophet speaking in the name of God, the trees are figures of speech for people.

In the eyes of Jesus too people are like trees, at least insofar as they can grow to spiritual greatness in his kingdom.

The process of daily growth, whether of tree or people, is imperceptible, just as the ultimate size of the shrub is invisible in the mustard seed. The kingdom of God grows from within, by means of his hidden power. "The coming of the kingdom of God does not admit of observation" (Lk 17:20). Its paradoxical nature contains an "already" and a "not yet," but from start to finish it is principally a spiritual kingdom because of "the godlike seed which has been sown" in humanity (Constitution on the Church in the Modern World, #3). That godlike seed is faith.

To learn to appreciate the "small-great" contrast in the kingdom of God, we're to start with its low order of insignificance, as it is among us or within us—the seed of faith. It will look impressive to us only at its finish.

Life for Jesus and his ministry are small, insignificant, localized in Bethlehem, Nazareth, Palestine. At his finish on the cross, when Jesus goes down to defeat, the smallness reappears.

Only Jesus' triumph over the grave, his resurrection, brings out its greatness, like a seed sprouting out of the ground. St. Clement of Rome, in his first letter to the Corinthians, refers to the ways God reveals the resurrection of Jesus as the culmination of what is to be. "Let us look at the resurrection in regard to the seasons." The difference between spring and fall, summer and winter, night and day, demonstrates start and finish. The power of divine providence, protecting the kingdom of God from ruin, is to be seen in the change from planting to harvesting.

No stages of growth outline the kingdom, like the GNP or the Dow Jones stock market report. A tentative description of the process of growth stems from other sources. Traditionally, spiritual writers have traced out the three ways of the spiritual life: purgative, illuminative, unitive. The purgative is the way of weeding out whatever prevents growth; the illuminative is the use of light and energy, the agents which make for much progress in virtue; and the unitive marks the harvest season.

To that great spiritual writer, St. John of the Cross, the figure of the mustard seed suggests a double use, negative and positive. "Evil grows into a large tree, a slight error in the beginning is a great one in the end." But growth into an immense tree of faith is possible to humans too, if they look for help from the Lord of the kingdom. "Pause a while and know that I am God" (Ps 46:10). For a starter John of the Cross recommends, "Learn to be empty of all things—interiorly and exteriorly—and you will behold that I am God."

We're not about to cut the mustard unless we take Jesus at his word. "I tell you solemnly, if your faith were the size of a mustard seed you could say to this mountain, 'Move from here to there,' and it would move; nothing would be impossible for you" (Mt 17:20). Faith in the kingdom of God is the mustard seed that achieves greatness. With "faith in all its fullness," the mustard seed is able "to move mountains" (1 Cor 13:2).

21

NO POUND OF FLESH

Mt 18:23-35

In the Shakespearean comedy, *The Merchant of Venice*, Portia, a noble and wise lady, disguises herself as the judge in the case of Shylock, the Jew, suing a Christian, Antonio. Portia, in love with Antonio, pleads mercy for him and explains why to Shylock.

> The quality of mercy is not strained,
> It droppeth as the gentle rain from heaven
> Upon the place beneath. It is twice blest;
> It blesseth him that gives, and him that takes.
> 'Tis mightiest in the mightiest. It becomes
> The throned monarch better than his crown . . .
> It is an attribute of God himself,
> And earthly power doth then show likest God's
> When mercy seasons justice. Therefore Jew
> Though justice be thy plea, consider this,
> That in the course of justice none of us
> Should see salvation. We do pray for mercy,
> And that same prayer doth teach us all to render
> The deeds of mercy.

Shylock wants his pound of flesh from Antonio anyhow, but Portia reminds him that legally he's allowed his pound of flesh from Antonio's breast but not a drop of blood. Shylock of course realizes the absurdity of trying to cut out flesh without spilling a drop of blood. The eventual settlement of the case leaves him lucky enough to keep his own life.

Shakespeare may have had in mind a verse from Sirach, "Mercy is welcome in time of trouble, like rain clouds in time of drought" (35:26). At any rate, Portia's plea for mercy parallels the real-life question that Peter puts to Jesus—whether forgiveness has to be given 7 or 77 times. The quality of mercy is what counts, Jesus answers.

Moreover, he pits two debtors against each other. The first is so deeply in debt to a king that he really can't settle his account. He has an enormous amount to repay, like our national debt or a zillion dollars. Seeing that he demands payment even at the cost of family—wife and children, we must surmise the king is a Gentile. The case isn't possible under Judaic law which forbids the sale of an Israelite family except for theft. The debtor prostrates himself before the king and promises the impossible, to work off the debt. Out of pity and acting magnanimously the king cancels the debt.

The first debtor turns around and tries to extort payment of a trivial sum from a fellow debtor. He feels no pity, shows no mercy, even though the repayment is impossible. When the king gets wind of this, he has him brought in to make amends. His reproach to the debtor has universal implications: "Were you not bound, then, to have pity on your fellow servant just as I had pity on you?"

Representing God, the king gets angry at how pitiless the first debtor has been. Pity always underlies mercy. Otherwise there's no standard but justice to go by in a case of debt or injury of any kind. God does indeed rule the world by two standards, mercy and justice, if not in time then on a day of reckoning in his kingdom. Jesus forewarns humankind against such a day of accountability, when it has to settle for its sinfulness. Justice is nothing to trifle with. At the final judgment, if we, as the first debtor, stand only by our just rights, God will revoke his mercy, for lack of sincere and wholehearted forgiveness on our part.

By estimating the enormity of sinfulness throughout human history, we begin to see how impossible it is for us as a people to square our accounts with God. To make up to God for the huge accumulation of sin is, humanly speaking, an impossibility. That's why the God of mercy out of pity wipes out our debt of sinfulness in the name of Jesus the Savior.

In *The Merchant of Venice*, Portia presents to Shylock the Jew the Christian doctrine of salvation through the mercy of God. The Jewish Scriptures are full of passages recommending mercy, especially chapter 28 of Sirach, and most especially verse 2: "Forgive your neighbor the hurt he does you, and when you pray, your sins will be forgiven." Hence Portia's approach isn't out of order. The Jews do believe in the doctrine of salvation for the faithful Jew.

The evangelist Matthew is very much in tune with the Jewish tradition and worship as he emphasizes mercy throughout his gospel and harmonizes it with other beatitudes: "Happy the merciful: they shall have mercy shown them"(5:7).

Divine mercy produces a willingness to forgive, a mercy flowing over for us to share with others. "Be compassionate as your Father is compassionate. . . . Grant pardon, and you will be pardoned. Give, and there will be gifts for you: a full measure, pressed down, shaken together, and running over . . . " (Lk 6:36-38).

For the sinner to accept divine mercy and then, backsliding, to act even more perversely, is to flaunt God the King.

To forgive some but not others is to spill blood while demanding a pound of flesh.

God deals with each of us, one by one, and not just universally. He "treats each one of us as if there were but one of us." The most appealing property of his mercy is "its dependence on time and place, person and circumstance, in other words, its tender discrimination" (Cardinal Newman).

Jesus surveys Judas from head to foot, searches him through and through, pleads with him again and again. And, even in the end, he addresses him as friend and by the personal name of Judas.

22

FIGS AND FERTILITY

Lk 13:6-9

In the Palestinian springtime the shoots and leaves of the fig tree promise a good harvest and betoken hope. So the sight of a barren fig tree leaves a twinge of sadness in the human heart, like the effect of infertility on a Hebrew wife.

I wasn't particularly hungry for figs in my three experiments of growing fig trees. My first attempt took place on a hillside about 32 miles northwest of Washington, D.C. For some unaccountable reason, the fig tree never took root after transplanting and died within a season. The second tree was a gift, a gesture of kindness and friendship from a grand old man who had nurtured it in his back yard. It thrived throughout the summer in its new setting, but with the oncoming of winter it had to be bedded in, wrapped and tied snuggly. It would have survived had not mice eaten off its bark and killed it. The third was grown indoors and produced two quarts of figs seasonally. The three trees haven't been worth a fig, though I have yet to curse a fig tree!

The fig tree in the gospel of Luke has a detail not to be found in my experiments nor in the Matthean or Markan version. Jesus is *hungry* when he spots a fig tree in full leaf but fruitless. He's hungry for figs only figuratively. In reality he's looking to people for the fruit of good works. He can't let the tree stand much longer, for in the midst of vines it saps too much energy from the soil, like his followers who expect him to feed them but produce no works of faith.

Jesus curses the fig tree, "May no one ever eat from you again" and keeps it barren (Mk 11:14). Later he and his disciples pass by the fig tree and see it withered to its roots (11:20). Symbolically, the fig tree (Israel) is as barren as the temple of Jerusalem is devoid of good works when Jesus casts the money-changers out of it (and acts out his parable).

The fig tree "leaves" the wrong impression. Outwardly it seems to be in good health, like the flourishing business in the Jerusalem temple; inwardly it is dying. Because it's so native to the land of Palestine, the prophets of old made use of it figuratively. Joel foresees prosperity for Israel, when "the trees bear fruit, vine and fig trees yield abundantly" (2:22). But the messianic prosperity follows only after the vines are laid waste, fig trees torn to pieces, stripped clean white and cut down (1:7).

God is the owner of the vineyard and fig tree, as the Lord of creation. "Yes," says Isaiah, "the vineyard of Yahweh Sabaoth is the House of Israel, and the men of Judah that chosen plant" (5:7). Hosea sees the ancestors of Israel as the "early fruit on the fig tree," and at first it yields "plenty of fruit" (9:10; 10:1).

On the other hand, Jeremiah calls Israel "a degenerate plant" which has no excuse for its barrenness (2:21). "I would like to go harvesting, says Yahweh. But there are no grapes on the vine, no figs on the fig tree: even the leaves are withered" (8:13).

The prophet has a vision of two baskets of figs, one prefiguring Israel, the other Judah. "The one basket contained excellent figs, like those that ripen first; the other very bad figs, so bad they were uneatable" (24:2). In the time of Jeremiah, the people left behind during the deportation to Babylon in 597 B.C. think themselves blessed. Actually the people in exile will turn out to be the true Israel. Why? Because, as Yahweh says through his prophet, "My eyes will watch over them for their good . . . to build them up and not to break them down, to plant them and not to tear them up. I will give them a heart to acknowledge that I am Yahweh. They shall be my people and I will be their God, for they will return to me with all their heart" (24:6-7).

Israel, its opportunity lost, is supplanted by the new Israel, the Church. The new people of God, like fig trees, are to "produce the appropriate fruit" (Mt 3:8). Like the prophets of old, Jesus is hungry for the fruit of the fig tree. It would seem that he's knowledgeable about the horticulture of his land. That like all fruit trees in Palestine, the fig has already been allowed to grow for three years. That its time is running short. That in the fourth year its fruit should be consecrated to God, and only in the fifth year may fruit be plucked from it and eaten (cf. Lv 19:23-25).

The Church is to produce a people of faith, Christians in the true sense of the word. They draw fruit—the good works of faith—from the tree of faith. They too are provided for in salvation history with an opportunity for productivity. "For every tree," says Jesus, "can be told by its own fruit: people do not pick figs from thorns . . . A good man draws what is good from the store of goodness in his heart; a bad man draws what is bad from the store of badness. For a man's words flow out of what fills his heart" (Lk 6:44-45).

At the end of his novel, *Monsignor Quixote*, Graham Greene narrates the visit of the hero and his Communist friend to the vineyard of Señor Diego where they can buy the best wine. Señor Diego finds out that one of his customers is a monsignor and invites the two to sit down at a table under a fig tree to dine on ham and wine, red and white. He complains to them that the rich Mexicans buy his best wine, mix it with bad wine, and sell it at a profit. Their priests let them get away with it. They're compensated by the Mexican rich when the latter bid for the statue of Our Lady, with all the money going to the priests.

Monsignor Quixote is vexed by the report. With ham and wine under his belt, he's bolstered against the "money-changers" and what he terms a "blasphemy." His attempt to stop the blasphemy merits him a mortal blow to the head.

Under the symbol of the fig tree, Monsignor Quixote produces the last of his good works. Then, in whatever it was—sleep? delirium? madness?—the monsignor places his fingers like a Host on the tongue of the Communist Mayor, his friend. So, through sacrifice, are all Christians to yield the fruit for which Jesus is hungry.

23

A CASE AT COURT

Lk 18:1-8

Our bishop, in his questionnaire regarding the status of women in society and in the Church, asked the diocese in what ways we thought women were excluded, alienated, discriminated against, or oppressed. It was like asking whether the widow was treated unfairly by the judge in her case at his court. Similarly, the answers, though not necessarily the most fitting to today's question, have something to say to all who suffer injustice and are kept poor thereby.

Besides the widow, three principal characters appear before us: her adversary, the judge, and God. The characters all have strong qualities, and the case has a happy resolution.

The first impression of the widow is of a rather elderly woman, but that may be wrong in respect to the life and times of Jesus. Possibly she's a young widow, the marriageable age for girls being between 13 and 14. Widowed, she belongs to what we call the marginalized of our society. Perhaps she's impoverished; certainly she's oppressed. She personifies all who "hunger and thirst for what is right" (Mt 5:6), that is, for justice in God's kingdom encompassing the Church and society.

Does she feel powerless as some women do nowadays who face unjust legal, social and religious structures and institutions?

Such institutions and structures are personified by the judge. The wrongs in them belong to somebody. They shouldn't be passed off impersonally. One resort for the widow is bribery, but she has no wherewithal to bribe the judge, and that, moreover, would be heaping one injustice on another. Her only resort is to insist upon her claim, to persist in her plea until the judge capitulates.

Suppose her adversary is a wealthy and influential man. Then she has even a tougher lawsuit on her hands, pitting the poor against the rich. Apparently it involves a money matter, the payment of a debt or an inheritance. Her plea hints at this, for she stands before a single judge who himself has the power to handle the case, or is appointed to it.

He's an inconsiderate, godless man. His soliloquy reveals his character and attitude toward the widow. We hear what he's thinking—that he doesn't care what people say about him. Gradually he's losing patience with the widow who by her nagging is getting on his nerves and eventually will wear him out. He submits to her in distress not for *her* good but out of a selfish motive, *his* own quiet and peace.

Only at its conclusion does God enter into the case, the judge who will vindicate all who seek justice. He's the final court of appeal, because originally in human affairs he sets the scales for what's right and what's wrong. Speaking in the name of God, Jesus joins the psalmist and the social-minded prophets who declaim against the "mockery of justice," against all who "carry on blindly, undermining the very basis of earthly society" (82:2, 5). On the other hand, "Yahweh, forever faithful, gives justice to those denied it . . . he keeps the orphan and widow" (146:6, 7, 9). God has a concern for the poor and hears their cry. Although pleas for justice may go unheard by human authority, God listens.

He will see to justice and act speedily. The divine justice on which Jesus hinges his promise is so easily skipped over:

". . . they shall be satisfied." We can either be confident or lose heart in his promise. But if we lose heart, we miss a major clue in the case of the widow, namely, the certainty of divine power, goodness and justice. And this certainty establishes a basis for persistent prayer.

A further detail shows up between God and the unjust judge. The judge grows weary of listening. God answers prayers that grow long. Should human justice fail, divine justice won't, even if it has to arrive at long last.

The thrust of the case gets at an attitude Christians ought to have in prayer. It presupposes that people do pray, just as truly as they bring a plea to court, when they think they have a just suit and a chance of winning. They'll refer a case from a lower to a higher court in a continuing appeal for justice. The widow exemplifies perseverance, which prevails on the judge as it does on God. She keeps on coming despite the odds against her, which is what perseverance is all about during the long delays in the administration of justice. Hence "the need to pray continually and never lose heart."

In support of perseverance, no concession is made to dropouts from prayer or worship. Like the poor widow, the Church at prayer is widowed from Christ so long as her sojourn on earth lasts. She remains the poor Church and the Church of the poor. Yet the risen and ascended Christ retains for her an unbreakable covenant of love and fidelity.

Under long trial, persecution, and disappointment, some people are tempted to fall away from the Church. Some persons feel they're not getting a fair hearing in the Church and slip away from her; others find her precepts hard to keep. The early symptom of such abandonment is wearying at prayer and stopping to beg for rights which accrue from baptism in the Church.

As an example of how possible it is to combine prayer with an appeal for justice, the Vatican II document on religious life admonishes: "Let the members of communities energetically cultivate the spirit of prayer and the practice of it," taking the Scripture and the liturgy, "especially the most holy mystery of the Eucharist, with hearts and voices attuned to the Church" (#6). The document calls for an interpenetration of the active and contemplative life, with the entire apostolic activity animated and suffused by a religious spirit (#8).

In the tradition of the Church, religious women and men, not unlike widows who plead at court (or give of their last penny), are to prolong and persist in prayer against all the unjust adversaries and judges in society.

24

PENNY-WISE, POUND-FOOLISH

Mt 25:1-13

It was a custom years ago, and perhaps still is in some localities, to serenade newlyweds with a mock serenade. Friends of the couple gathered after the wedding to hail them with kettles, horns, pans and other noisemakers. The racket—it was just that to anybody's ears—sounded throughout the neighborhood. Tin cans strung together and tied to the back bumper of the wedding car, clanged along as it drove off for their honeymoon.

This part of the post-wedding celebration, a playful stunt, did little for the couple but call public attention to their marriage. It was a far cry from the torchlight procession of the ten bridesmaids that took place *before* the wedding ceremony, without noisemaking, at the time of our Blessed Lord.

Wedding practices have come a long way. As a matter of fact, there was a variety of Palestinian wedding customs when the nuptial event took place during the day. All of them included dancing and other entertainment which came to a halt at night, before the ceremony.

That explains why the bridesmaids had to carry the torches in a procession. Their torches were made of sticks wrapped with oil-soaked rags burning and lighting up the way. Both bride and bridegroom were led by the bridesmaids to the home of the bridegroom's parents where the ceremony was to be held.

First they went to the home of the bride and accompanied her, then they did the same for the bridegroom who may have been delayed by the negotiations with the bride's parents over the gifts he was to exchange for his bride. A long delay indicated he had to offer a good deal for his bride, so highly was she thought of.

The bridesmaids dozed off, presumably tired out by the pre-nuptial festivities. Once awake, the first five wisely supplied themselves with enough oil to last indefinitely into the night. The second five were shortsighted; they ran out of oil and wasted time in procuring more of it. They had the door closed against them, excluding them from the wedding ceremony itself.

Perhaps the supply of oil doesn't impress us as a source of light as much as it did the Israelite communities. Israel had a great appreciation for oil. It was drawn from the olive trees which grew aplenty on the land, providing them with not only fuel for light, but with food and ointment as well. With empty lamps, the foolish bridesmaids would have to grope in the dark. Were they what we might call penny-wise but pound-foolish?

Their story is one of the seven so-called parousia parables in the gospel of Matthew. Like the other six it contains three themes: that the Messiah is coming for judgment day; that the time of his arrival is unforeseeable; and that there's need for preparation. Like tragedies, the parousia parables can end unhappily.

The implication here is that the Messiah plays the role of the bridegroom. Jesus, the Messiah, has a piece of advice to give, to alert us to a crisis—his Second Coming. Since the time of his return is unpredictable, he wants us to be ready for it. He emphasizes the necessity of the preparation but sets no deadline for it. He doesn't commit himself to any day or hour: he may be slow or fast in coming. The interval between his first and second coming is what we now experience. His kingdom to come hinges upon the judgment he will render, which is irrevocable once the door to the kingdom is closed, as the door was for the foolish bridesmaids who arrived too late.

Collectively the bridesmaids symbolize the Church, the Bride of Christ, or, on the local level, every Christian community. Whether the communities turn out to be wise or foolish depends on their degree of readiness. The apostle Paul, matchmaker for the communities he visits on his journeys, is afraid of interference in their marriage with Christ. "I arranged for you to marry Christ, so that I might give you away as a chaste virgin to this one husband" (2 Cor 11:2). Paul fears that the Church, like Eve, may be deceived by Satan speaking through false preachers who proclaim a new Jesus. The Church then is led into a wrong marriage.

The "day" and the "hour" for which the Church is to stay awake sounds an alarm, like a clock. In the gospel of Matthew they are key words connoting Christ's coming in judgment. Warned by faith about the Bridegroom who is to come, she should be ever-watchful. She has been duly forewarned about not just the big crisis of the last judgment but the daily temptation to squander time. After the early Church's experience of the Bridegroom's delay, procrastination is all the more tempting since he seems to be in no hurry to return.

Caught in the celebration preliminary to the wedding, as the foolish bridesmaids were, we may budget no time to replenish our lamps with oil. The time left in this world before the judgment may run short. We need to take precautionary measures before proceeding farther to a meeting with the Bridegroom.

The Church as the Bride of Christ has the custom of keeping a sanctuary lamp continually lit at her altars, tables of celebration. She derives this custom from Yahweh's instruction to Moses and the people of Israel, that they should bring "pure olive oil for the light, and to keep a flame burning there (in the Tent of Meeting with him) perpetually" (Ex 27:20). If we allow the lamp to burn out, will God see it as a sign we have let him pass out of our life, that we no longer care to cherish his presence and power? Is it a sign also that we haven't kept up a faith-filled life of prayer, that at some point we have given up vigilance?

Wise is the Church in keeping a lamp burning at her altars and the light of faith witnessing to the arrival of her Bridegroom. The celebrations at her altars won't detain her but hasten the coming of her Beloved.

25

ALL IS GIFT

Lk 17:7-10

It may sound like the start of a self-help quiz, this question Jesus asks about the value of human acts, in order to determine human worth by a human standard and then try to see the same from a divine viewpoint. His question isn't easy to answer; it has been discussed, disagreed upon and argued over from time immemorial among the various Christian denominations. In discussion it has been framed this way: Are we saved by good works or by faith or by both?

A first principle to gauge work by is justice. The principle at stake here is simply stated by Paul in his first letter to Timothy: "The worker deserves his pay" (5:18). But in Matthew the principle is stated less strongly: ". . . The workman deserves his keep" (10:10). Justice dictates that everybody should get what is due for work. But the application of justice is complicated by many factors. Justice argues for a living wage, which is hard to come by because of the inflationary cost of living. Moreover, women claim they should be paid the same as men for work of comparable worth. Then there is the matter of special benefits and bonuses, of profit-sharing, perks and pensions.

In our society labor or job opportunity is ruled by competition. It factors into almost every human endeavor, most especially into games, sports and other contests. But it isn't an American invention. It has a long history. The competitive spirit was first fostered by the Greeks, which Homer expressed in his poem *The Iliad*, "ever to be best and to surpass others," whether that be in races, athletics, oratory, music, dance, theater, or beauty contests. Lest we mistake it, the Greek competitive spirit was thought to be religious. Remember how the apostle Paul, as his life drew to a close, saw himself as competitive in a Greco-Roman world: "I have fought the good fight to the end; I have run the race to the finish," for which a crown was reserved for him (2 Tm 4:7-8).

But if mere rivalry runs our races or contests for rewards, in our modern setting it has to be between ourselves and the false gods of materialism and secularism that can turn us away from the true God, the goal of our salvation. We aren't competing with one another for spiritual rewards or prizes or wages, nor should we be, nor did the saints of the past. They, in fact, left behind whatever surplus they had for the treasury of the Church. Their contributions to our salvation aid us beyond our calculations.

Saints, the servants of God, called to obey his will as his law commands, also need the benefit of his love and mercy. The divine law itself has built into it sanctions—reward or punishment. For its keeping, are we to be criticized for a legalistic mentality or a commercial spirit when we expect reward or merit or recompense?

If work, competition, law, seem to require some kind of remuneration, what are we to think of this conclusion to a job well done: "We are merely servants: we have done no more than our duty"? It certainly raises the questions of merit and indulgences. It needs further examination as to how it applies to modern times.

In antiquity, the servant had two chores to do, one was fieldwork—ploughing or tending sheep—and the other was housework. When he came in from the field, he still had housework to do, to prepare a meal for his master before taking his own. He had to tidy himself up first, which some translations explain as girding himself to prevent stumbling over his garment or soiling it.

Thinking over this master-servant relationship, it makes us wonder that no polite thanks was due to the servant. Strictly speaking, he received no thanks for a duty he had performed under command. Nor had he any claim to special gratitude. What then lies in the background of this question of gratitude?

Supposing the master did owe thanks to his servant, or that the latter demanded a token of gratitude, we begin to understand what Jesus was driving at. In his time there was a widespread expectation among Hebrews of special treatment from the Lord due to their status as his chosen people. There was prevalent a Pharisaic attitude that because they were chosen, they deserved reward. Jesus would have his listeners renounce the Pharisaic attitude of superiority and self-righteousness, as if they had some claim upon God.

As the people of God, we never earn a covenantal relationship to him, nor is he ever indebted to us. He sets up a covenant of love with us freely, of his own initiative, out of the superabundance of his heart. His goodness is diffusive of itself. Whatever our good works, whatever our sacrifices, whatever our achievements in life, whatever the long years of faithful service to him and his people, we have neither claim nor right to reward. Because all is gift from him, all is grace, we remain "unworthy servants."

If we expect the Lord to keep track of all the merits and indulgences we have "piled up" like bank accounts, investments, trust funds, or insurance policies, we do him an injustice. We really never get so far ahead in life spiritually, that we can live off a surplus. Do we not fall short at times of our own expectations? We can be content with the willingness to serve God selflessly.

St. Paul had this willingness at heart as he offered himself for the sake of Israel: "I would willingly be condemned and be cut off from Christ if it could help my brothers of Israel, my own flesh and blood" (Rm 9:3). Out of a spirit of love and mercy, Paul left himself open to the impossibility of assuming the guilt and punishment of Israel in a way similar to Christ who accepted suffering and death for the sake of us all.

Beggars, not choosers, of God's gifts, we pray repeatedly in the words of the First Eucharistic Prayer, "Do not consider what we truly deserve, but grant us your forgiveness." What God has in store for us he grants out of his goodness, loving kindness and mercy. And what the Church disburses is from the treasury of Christ and his saints, and not out of a strict sense of distributive justice.

Rather than adopt a greedy determination to squeeze out of God all we can, our intention in serving him is to be enriched "in the joy and gladness that come from an abundance of all things" (Dt 28:47). Why go bargain-hunting in a sort of spiritual supermarket owned and operated by God Incorporated?

26

Dangerous Riches

Lk 16:19-31

Listening to the same story from various storytellers, one can't help but note how it changes in the retelling. Storytellers alter details deliberately to suit themselves, or their memories lapse, or they fit stories to the circumstances of their hearers. Jesus the storyteller didn't hesitate to borrow stories for his own use, for example, the folktale of the rich man and Lazarus from Alexandrian (Egyptian) Jews.

The rich man was sharply contrasted with the poor man, and their situations switched from this life to the next. A stage director would have to set up two scenes or three to dramatize the situations. The many contrasts make for a livelier story: Abraham's bosom and Hades, agony and comfort, the drop of water and the magnificent feast, Moses and the prophets on the one hand and the risen dead on the other, God's verdict and the world's on the rich man and the poor man.

Poor Lazarus, lying at the gate of the rich man's estate, not only has to go hungry; he suffers from skin disease and gets it licked by dogs. Poverty and disease thrust upon him the reputation of a sinner punished by God. But Lazarus has the unique distinction of being the only character in Jesus' parables to have a proper name: Lazarus, which means "God helps." God does

103

help the poor in ways the rich can't: "The hungry he has filled with good things, the rich sent empty away" (Lk 1:53). The rich man is left nameless, nondescript, as if he has no character to speak of.

Food and drink, clothing, shelter—they all spell part of the difference between the two, rich and poor. "Rich man, poor man, beggarman, thief. . . ." There's no evidence that the rich man is a thief, that he came by his wealth dishonestly by defrauding the poor. But he's a rich spendthrift who can't claim that his material success and economic status are a sign of God's favor or a reward for virtue. The Pharisees living at the time of Jesus consider them to be such a sign.

Luxurious living may very easily blind the rich to their unloving attitude toward the poor, and their selfishness may even prevent them from believing in an afterlife and the retribution that it brings. The least they can do is to allow the poor beggar to eat the scraps of bread they let fall from the table after soaking and cleansing their fingers with it in finger bowls. But they're unwilling to extend even this little gesture of kindness.

The rich-poor contrast is sharpened in the two states of the afterlife, Abraham's bosom and Hades. Abraham's bosom is a Hebrew figure of speech for the gathering of the Hebrew ancestors, Abraham in particular, after death (Jg 2:10). Lazarus is privileged to recline next to Abraham at table, while the rich man can claim no favor from his kinship with the patriarch. His love of money is no substitute for good works. Abraham shows him no pity; Lazarus isn't allowed to offer a drop of water to slake the rich man's thirst. The refusal suggests the severity of his suffering, and it recalls the earlier refusal of the rich man to let wine or water-soaked scraps of bread fall from his table.

A belief was held to in late Judaism that the dead had to wait in Sheol, the underworld, for the general resurrection. That the good and the evil, during their intermediate state, could see each other after death, across the gulf between Abraham's bosom and Hades. The gulf was unbridgeable, beyond trespass, and the judgment committing the rich man and the poor man to the two sides was irrevocable.

In the rich man's dialogue with Abraham, the former pleads with the latter for both his own relief and the rescue of his five brothers. He repeats the plea, "Father Abraham," intending his kinship with his forefather to gain him privilege. Doesn't it sound to you as if the rich man is trying to curry favor with Abraham? The latter lets him know that should the five brothers refuse to listen to Moses or the prophets, whose message is clear and forceful enough, not even a warning from the dead would impress them.

The Christian belief in the afterlife teaches us who are living on this side of death three things: that there's no possibility of return to life in space and time; that the afterlife can't continue this life with its space-time dimensions; and that there's a future awaiting us, which is the first and final of its kind, for Jesus doesn't precede us in death into nothingness, even though death breaks all our present-day attachments to things and persons.

All of this fantastic detail goes to show that Jesus shares the apocalyptic ideas of his contemporaries. Yet his intention isn't to describe conditions in the afterlife. Nor is he a hellfire preacher; he hardly speaks of hell.

He simply signals a warning about the final judgment to come, that it will be against the unrepentant. There's still time to decide for or against him. Jesus calls for resolute action in due time.

The rich-poor gulf in this life, which the American bishops broach in their pastoral letter on Catholic Social Teaching and the U.S. Economy, is an issue for us to decide about and try to resolve. The rich and developed countries lord their position and power over the poor Third World countries. The rich of our own country lord it over our poor. Whatever unjust separation lies between the two, cries for justice. The will to rectify the injustice arrives too late in the afterlife. Lazarus may very well be taken to personify the poor nations of the world who suffer from inconsideration, injustice and foreign exploitation.

The bishops write in their pastoral letter: "In Luke alone Jesus tells the parable of the rich man who does not see the poor and suffering Lazarus at his gate" (16:19-31). When the rich man finally "sees" Lazarus, the opportunity for conversion has passed into the place of torment. Pope John Paul II has often recalled this parable to warn the prosperous not to be blind to the great poverty that exists beside the great wealth. In any case, wealth is no help, nor is poverty a hindrance in the order of salvation.

27

TOWERS AND SKYSCRAPERS

Lk 14:28-30

An unfinished, abandoned project, a house or shed where a prospector and his family intended to settle down, leaves a tinge of sadness. The only thing left of their project is the foundation, a monument to an aborted business. Or this one house, incomplete, on Lark Street nearby, in a neighborhood of so many beautiful homes. It appears so out of place with the others, themselves so well designed and constructed. A pity, too, for whoever could neither finish nor sell the property. It has been standing there, an empty shell, for over two years. Its "For Sale" sign adds a touch of irony to the whole scene.

Although Jesus didn't reveal why he chose the example of the unfinished tower, it must have come to his mind because he lived and worked amid vineyards where the tower was a fairly common sight, like a farm building or barn that overlooked the land. A large building, it could serve for housing, too, as suggested by the high cost of the foundation. Its builder didn't get beyond the foundation, not high-rise enough for use as a watchtower against thieves or robbers in his vineyard.

The theme of construction arose early in the history of Israel and was an important "blueprint" in the Bible. It began already in the book of Genesis: "Come, let us build ourselves a town and a tower with its top reaching heaven" (11:4). It was natural for Israel in its life-situation to be creative; in the process of settling down in Canaan after a nomadic life, the people had to build houses, temples, city-states. In fact, a natural human trait is to be creative, skyscraping. Architects, artisans and craftspeople testify to what a sense of satisfaction they derive from creative construction.

Consider the feeling of initiating a project and failing to finish it. My mother used to advise me as a boy, never start something you can't finish. Jesus' question, "Which of you here?" is a Semitic test case briefly asking for a self-evaluation, for a personal judgment on how one would decide about the project of the tower builder.

To be better informed, the disciple of Christ has to weigh this earlier statement of his, warning against taking discipleship lightheartedly: "Anyone who does not carry his cross and come after me cannot be my disciple" (Lk 14:27). How much can one carry in the following of Christ? One must undergo a test, like a trial run or novitiate, to find out that discipleship demands detachment, tribulation and suffering.

Soren Kierkegaard, the existentialist philosopher, recalls the tower builder in his *The Gospel of Suffering*. "Before a man begins something, whether it involves acting or suffering, he first makes an estimate as to whether, if he acts, he can construct a tower, and how high; whether, if he suffers, he has the energy to build, after all, and how fundamentally. Consequently, he makes an estimate of his strength, and the relationship between his strength and the task; he *ponders* on this. To ponder is a figurative expression, but very significant, and therefore it has the advantage that a figurative expression always has, that, as through a secret door, aye, as by a sudden stroke of magic, from the most commonplace conception, one is standing in the midst of supreme conceptions, so that one suddenly discovers, when one is talking about the simple, daily matters, he is also talking about supreme matters" (p. 118).

To ponder is synonymous with what Jesus says when he tells us to "first sit down and work out the cost" of discipleship. To ponder is to weigh, reflect, plan. Discipleship is composed of temporal and eternal "materials." The life and development of a disciple is like the construction of a tower. Figuring only on the temporal, without giving any thought to the eternal, is like calculating only the foundation without a careful and complete assessment of the whole of life, a supreme matter.

One who leaves life an unfinished business, the temporal without the eternal, incurs the butt of ridicule. "Here is a man who started to build and was unable to finish."

Was Jesus, who had his followers "sit down and work out the cost" of discipleship, a religious fanatic, insisting too much on a temporal, human commitment? Did he require of others what he himself was unable to fulfill? Robert Graves, the English poet and classical scholar, titled a book in 1946, *King Jesus*, and startled Christians with his interpretation that Jesus died not on the cross but a natural death as a Jewish layman. Contrariwise, Kierkegaard saw the suffering of Christ as superhuman; with a superhuman patience Christ hung upon the towering cross. Thus a discipleship entailing great patience and endurance shouldn't surprise us.

Is it at all possible to foresee what an entire building project will cost nowadays, with so unstable an economy? And so many cost overruns? Jesus proposes no economic forecast but a moral and spiritual foresight. Look before you leap. Think things through. Pursue a building project thoughtlessly and you run a risky business. Impetuosity and get-rich-quick schemes cause trouble. The construction of a complete Christian life takes foresight, a vision beyond the temporal to the eternal.

Wisely, the psalmist takes this long-range view: "If Yahweh does not build the house, in vain the masons toil" (127:1). Yahweh promises help to Israel on its return from exile: "My eyes will watch over them for their good, to bring them

back to this land, to build them up and not to break them down
. . ." (Jr 24:6). The same promise extends to the new Israel, the
Church: "You are God's building . . . Everyone doing the
building must work carefully. For the foundation, nobody can
lay any other than the one which has already been laid, that is
Jesus Christ" (1 Cor 3:9-11).

Suppose, however, through circumstances beyond our control and through some miscalculation, and after a false start, it's
humanly impossible to finish a work. Can't God reconstruct a
life, a building? Yes, God can rebuild a people, a city. "I build you
once more; you shall be rebuilt, virgin of Israel . . . See, the days
are coming—it is Yahweh who speaks—when the city of
Yahweh will be rebuilt . . ." (Jr 31:4, 38). Human failure doesn't
rule out the reconstruction, the upbuilding possible to the Lord.

28

PIED - PIPERS
Mt 11:16-19;   Lk 7:31-35

A centuries-old, German folk tale, centers on a hero who rid the town of Hamelin of rats. It was popularized by the English poet Robert Browning in a poem titled "The Pied Piper of Hamelin." Hamelin was a pleasant spot by the river Weser until it was infested with rats, forcing the townsfolk to flock to the townhall and appeal to the mayor and his council for rat extermination. The town officials, typically political, were taking it easy but had to do something about the rat crisis, or else the townsfolk would throw them out of office.

They were racking their brains for a remedy when the strangest looking fellow entered their council chamber. Nobody knew who he was or where he came from. Tall and lean, he wore a coat colored half red, half yellow, with a scarf to match. The pipe hanging from the scarf's end and the quaint clothes he wore, gave him his name, Pied Piper. He had a secret charm, so he said, "And I chiefly use my charm / On creatures that do people harm. . . ." He volunteered to free the town of rats for 1000 guilders. The mayor and his council were only too glad to hire him for 50,000.

The Piper went into the street, blew only three shrill notes, and the entire rat population appeared—grumbling, rumbling,

111

tumbling. From street to street he piped them out and led them into the river Weser where they drowned, all but one left to tell the story of Rat-land. When the Pied Piper stepped up to collect his money, the officials remembered their expensive council dinners, grew economical in a hurry, reneged on their promise, and paid the Pied Piper only 50 guilders.

Disappointed with them of course, the Piper threatened, "And folks who put me in a passion / May find me pipe after another fashion." The bold mayor spoke up, "You threaten us, fellow? Do your worst, / Blow your pipe till you burst!"

The Piper returned to the street and piped sweet, soft notes that brought out all the little children—rustling, bustling, justling, hustling, pattering, clattering, clapping, and chattering. He led them all to a mountainside, bypassing the river. He would never be able to lead them over the mountaintop, the townspeople thought. But a mountainside door opened and let them all in, all but one who was too lame to dance all the way behind the Pied Piper. The lame boy was left alone, sad, because he too had been promised entry into a joyous land.

The mayor sent out word for the Piper to return with the children and offered him "silver and gold to his heart's content," but the Piper and the child dancers were gone forever. Their story was inscribed on a column and painted on a great church window, in their memory. To this day there's a tribe who have outlandish ways and dress.

According to this old legend and the Browning poem, a pied piper is someone who induces others to imitate his example especially but not necessarily by false or extravagant promises. Who of us doesn't occasionally act like a pied piper? Jesus compares the people of his generation and himself, too, with a pied piper, both in the good and in the bad sense of the name.

Watch and listen to the children in the market place. Great imitators as they are, they wish to organize wedding and funeral games in the street. They ask their playmates to join them, the boys to dance as at weddings, the girls to play at a funeral game by burying a grasshopper. The games, merry and sad, involve them in quarrels; some children quarrel with others who refuse to join in the fun. Apparently the latter want to domineer the play. Spoilsports, they sulk along the sidelines. Like the Hamelin mayor and his council, or like the religious leaders in Jesus' generation, they want to run the show.

His generation can be compared to children, moody and fickle. They reject what God proposes to them, his message, whether joyful or somber. They hear neither the theme of repentance from John the Baptist nor the joyful news of salvation from Jesus. They regard John and Jesus as rebellious sons of Israel (cf. Dt 21:20). The one they call possessed, the other a glutton, drunkard, and keeper of bad company. Neither John nor Jesus can pipe the right tune. Nothing seems to please them; they must have their own way. Jesus suffers this opposition and criticism early in his public life.

He wonders why his generation is so sulky: Why aren't the people in tune with the two pied pipers? Jesus projects an answer into the future: "Yet wisdom has been proved right by her actions" (Matthew), or, "by all her children" (Luke). The men and women of his time prove themselves wrong by refusing to cooperate with him. They're unworthy of him and unwise for not welcoming and appreciating his good news of salvation. Not dancing to his tune, they'll regret it and will have to listen to his cry of warning and announcement of judgment. His words echo the proverb: "And now . . . listen to me; listen to instruction and learn to be wise, do not ignore it" (Pr 8:32).

God, all-wise, has wise designs and values for his people. His wisdom is vindicated by events in the course of history—by the Christ-event, Christ being wisdom in Person, sharing in the attributes of God. His people become children of wisdom by recognizing and accepting him as the revelation of God.

In one sense, John the Baptist and Jesus were the pied

pipers of Palestine. Both piped a tune which the people of their day regretfully refused to hear.

In another sense, Christians as followers of Christ are pied pipers to their own generation. How do contemporaries react to the tunes we play to them? Do they dance along to the tune of Christian moral and spiritual values, mourn over the lack of wholesome values in society, or do they sulk like children who want their own way in the game of life?

Wisdom is the tune: We hear it from the children piping and playing in the market place, or from Jesus in the role of the pied piper. Only the wise teachings and deeds of those who follow Christ will prove Jesus to be right: "Unless you change and become like little children . . ." (Mt 18:3).

29

PROMISES TO KEEP

Mt 21:28-32

The opportunity presents itself to think over the dilemma of two sons and give your opinion of them. Clearly, Jesus would have you reflect and draw your own conclusion.

Each of the two sons is assigned a task in their father's vineyard. One doesn't volunteer to go, the other does. Evidently they talked it over among themselves before they considered his request carefully. They both have a change of mind and will. The first recants his no, the second refuses to go. The case is clear as to which of the two obeys.

The two sons represent two classes of people with whom Jesus has to associate. The first is the type of the tax collectors (the IRS of his day) and harlots or prostitutes who are regarded as the scum of society. Popular opinion of such professionals need not coincide with what God the Father or Jesus may think of them. Jesus befriends the tax collector Matthew, calling him into his close company. He is accused of being a glutton and drunkard and charged with associating with prostitutes. Incidentally, the letter to the Hebrews speaks well of the faith and good works of the harlot Rahab who in the story of Joshua protects the two spies about to reconnoiter the promised land of Canaan.

The second son is a type of Jesus' adversaries and critics

115

who eventually plan his death and have him executed. They're the religious leaders—the chief priests, elders and Pharisees who fail to live up to their responsibility. Jesus warns the people against following them: ". . . Do not be guided by what they do since they do not practice what they preach" (Mt 23:3).

His words are double-edged. He vindicates all the poor sinners who at first refuse to do the will of God the Father but then gradually repent and make their way into his kingdom. He rebukes the complacent Jewish leaders who claim to do God's will by obeying the Law of Moses, which they interpret to their ease and benefit. Not only in this circumstance but throughout his gospel, the evangelist Matthew takes issue with the Pharisees who neglect the trust of their religious office.

As he's projected in the Matthean gospel, Jesus throws a second punch at the Jewish leaders; he contrasts them with John the Baptist who practiced what he preached. The leaders went out to hear him but left unconvinced.

A possible Old Testament parallel, which the leaders should have been well-advised about, is the prophet Nathan's protest to King David in 2 S 12:1-7. It takes the form of a story about two men in the same town, the one rich, the other poor. The rich man has abundant flocks and herds, while the poor man has only one ewe lamb which he treats like a pet. When the former entertains a guest, he treats him with the lamb he robs from the poor man. The incident arouses David's sense of justice and provokes him to anger. But then Nathan tips the scales of justice against David himself who was so richly blessed by Yahweh and yet betrayed Uriah the Hittite. Caught off guard, David convicts himself and is justly reprimanded, "Why have you shown contempt for Yahweh, doing what displeases him?"

The father who gives orders to his two sons stands in for God the Father who asks obedience of his children. The vineyard he sends them to is the world. As children of God, baptized into his Christian family but still living in the world as our temporary home, we have promises to keep. Religious promises differ by far from political promises and platforms often made to win votes. They bind us to do the will of God, not simply win his favor. The fulfillment of such promises prove us to be doers and not just sayers of his word. "It is not those who say to me, 'Lord, Lord,' who will enter the kingdom of heaven, but the person who does the will of my father in heaven" (Mt 7:21).

The two sons and their responses accentuate the difference between true and false Christianity. True belief in the word of God as preached by John the Baptist and Jesus confirms itself in true Christian practice. The reason Christians refuse to do the will of the heavenly Father is that they don't truly believe in Jesus. The test of faith is the true Christian life.

Children of God, we profess the truths of our faith in an act of worship, but the faith itself is put to test in the service of our neighbor. Vice versa, the test of faith for those who claim to do good to their neighbor comes in the worship of God. Worship of God and service of neighbor must go together like clasped hands, in mutual support. Or else we shouldn't excuse ourselves of the same fault Jesus accused the religious leaders of, the disparity between the way we treat God and the way we treat our neighbor.

Once we make a promise to God, we have a pledge to neighbor to keep. How does the one obligation involve the other? In the same way that the father binds his two sons to work in a vineyard, a *place* of responsibility. Its produce is food and drink for others *and* a fulfillment of the father's will. We children of God, at work in the vineyard of the Lord, his Church, have promises to keep.

Robert Frost, the American poet, has suggested in his poems a sense of place coupled with a feeling for people. The lyric truth in his meditative poem titled "Stopping by Woods on a Snowy Evening" arrives at a climax regarding responsibility and obligations to be fulfilled. The poem pictures a woods with a farmhouse owned by a villager. Sleigh rider and horse stop by the woods and lake to drink in the atmosphere of the place. The poet is briefly moved by his experience of the sound and sight of a snowfall:

> The woods are lovely, dark and deep,
> But I have promises to keep,
> And miles to go before I sleep.
> And miles to go before I sleep.

With a promise we enforce the heavenly call to work in the vineyard of the Lord. The ordinary, daily obligation to God's call and command may seem trivial, yet it has a binding force over a lifetime because it entails the will of God. No doubt, we do have other, more serious Christian promises to keep, bound up first of all with our baptismal vows, which last for a lifetime. Additionally binding for many Christians are marriage or religious vows. We shouldn't make up our minds and wills about them, or change them, willy-nilly and still expect a place in the kingdom of God.

30

THE WHEELER- DEALER

Lk 16:1-8

In Galilee, where Jesus did some of his preaching, there were some rich, absentee landlords (like wealthy landowners in our country who have tenant farmers). A business crisis arose which Jesus had no part in, leaving to Caesar his own things. The economic situation, however, indicates that he was an observer of Palestinian business life while professing no expertise in it.

Similarly, the American bishops start their pastoral letter on Catholic Social Teaching and the U.S. Economy with questions about economic life: "Every perspective on economic life that is human, moral, and Christian must be shaped by three questions: What does the economy *do* for people? What does it do *to* people? And how do people *participate* in it?" (I, 1). The same questions possibly apply to the life situation of the crafty but dishonest manager Jesus refers to.

Admittedly, it's rather unusual for him to take a criminal and crook as an example. The real charge against the manager or steward is that he's "wasteful" of property not his own. His is a case of embezzlement, in more technical language. Entrusted with another's property, he commits a breach of trust by failing to turn over money or property to whom it rightfully belongs. Misappropriating goods, he's caught in the act or practice of

119

stealing and has to give a total account of his stewardship. Found guilty, he's fired.

The account the manager has to give calls our attention to the economic situation the American bishops point to in our country and the world over. The manager dealt in oil and wheat which were, along with wine, the staple food and drink of the Palestinian people. (Food and agriculture are among the economic issues the American bishops select and express concern for, for which they seek a just policy.) The manager was tampering with what the bishops term "the essential human needs of society," and wasn't meeting them equitably. The bishops write, "But these goods—the foundation of God's gift of life—are too crucial to be taken for granted."

Nowadays we understand stewardship to be the management of time, talent, and treasure—not much differently from the economic situation in the time of Jesus. Apparently the steward or manager doesn't have much time to settle accounts with his master's debtors. They're handed something similar to promissory notes which have to be paid back by a deadline, in kind rather than in money. The manager with the talent for it sizes up his situation. He knows his talent, and his candor helps him out here and now. Physically unable to dig, too embarrassed to beg, he still has to ensure security for his future. Hence he has to use foresight and act decisively.

Despite his past crookedness, in this critical moment he decides and acts cleverly, thus providing himself a way out. The debtors are to write out their bills, perhaps to prevent anyone from recognizing his own handwriting. He renegotiates, slashes their debts, though without dishonesty to his master. You see, he's entitled to skim off his own profit; he has a legal right as a sort of profit-sharer to reduce the debtors' amounts, for in reality he's foregoing his own profit. The amounts are cut down to about 150 olive trees and 100 acres of wheat—10 years of his average salary. He resorts to this bit of trading off in order to gain himself a welcome from his master's debtors. His resolute and enterprising action gets him out of a jam.

The American bishops call for this spirit of enterprise in the present-day economic situation. They urge "conscientious business people" to devise "new and more equitable ways to organize resources and the workplace" (#2). "People shape the economy and in turn are shaped by it" (#5). "The United States is among the most economically powerful nations on earth" (#6), but it has some unfinished business. "Persons in management face many hard choices each day, choices on which the well-being of many others depends" (#111). The bishops' letter goes on to say that managers are to be held to moral responsibility, because their resources are held in trust; they have not created capital (substitute "treasure") on their own. The old-time manager accomplishes in partnership with the debtors what managers are supposed to do today, that is, develop greater participation and accountability between labor and management.

Somehow, since we're all managers in the affairs of life, we can learn a lesson from the cleverness or astuteness of the manager. He could have been hesitant, wrung his hands in desperation, and waited for a solution. But he made up his mind and acted promptly, and therefore he was praised for his worldly wisdom. He was a child of this world; we're the children of light who are to use other-worldly wisdom in order to prepare for an other-worldly judgment. We stake our whole life on the promise of the kingdom, a kingdom so treasurable as to defy the imagination.

The last document of Vatican II, the *Constitution on the Church in the Modern World*, observes that humankind, like the manager, stands in a critical stage of history. How is it to manage its responsibility as the divinely appointed steward of creation "with justice and holiness" (#34)? Its stewardship is a trust over the things of nature which it betrays when it wantonly usurps, monopolizes, or exploits them. "Manifested at the beginning of time, the divine plan is that man should subdue the earth, bring creation to perfection, and develop himself" (#57). The clever and honest steward simultaneously keeps his account of creation in good order and places himself at the service of all the Master's debtors.

As managers of earthly affairs, we're to remain in the favor of God, his angels and saints. Responsible stewardship of time, talent, and treasure is a contemporary solution to problems—economic, political, moral and religious.

Up to date there has been considerable disagreement among Scriptural scholars as to whom Jesus was addressing himself. Was it to the Pharisees, his disciples, or a general audience? In any case, there was an original setting, then a later Church setting, as the concluding verses of the parable suggest. Presently we are to adapt ourselves and participate in current problems. We have no time, talent, or treasure to lose.

31

CHRISTUS VINCIT

Mk 3:22-30; Mt 12:24-32

Nazareth, his hometown, is the scene of Jesus' encounter with the Scribes. Their accusation against him is the second on record in the gospel of Mark. The first is that his relatives think he's out of his mind. The Scribes' accusation, the worse of the two, is that he's possessed by a devil. They perceive him as having "an unclean spirit," as teaming up with Satan. Thanks to this association, he has the power of casting out devils. Both accusations spring from a misunderstanding of the person and ministry of Jesus.

Jesus attempts to set the record straight about himself by speaking up to the Scribes. If his power to cast out devils comes from the prince of devils, then Satan is his own worst enemy and his rule or kingdom is divided against itself and can't last. He has mutiny in his ranks. And the same is true, on a smaller scale, of a household divided, like a family, neighborhood, or community quarreling. Rebellion threatens the end of the household, just as it does of Satan. Divide and conquer. Jesus and Satan make up a losing team.

In self-defense, Jesus draws on his past experience, his temptation and conflict with Satan in the desert, on the temple pinnacle, and on the mountaintop. His struggle with Satan is akin to that of a householder with a burglar who has to be able to overpower the householder and tie him up before he can burgle his house. Jesus, more powerful than his opponent, vanquishes him *before* his public ministry, *during* it, and at its *close*. He passes this power on to his seventy-two disciples, "I watched Satan fall like lightning from heaven. Yes, I have given you power to tread underfoot . . . the whole strength of the enemy" (Lk 10:17-19).

Shortly before his death Jesus predicted, "Now the prince of this world is to be overthrown" (Jn 12:31). The victories of Jesus and his disciples over Satan, by their exorcisms, anticipated Jesus' ultimate victory over him by his death on the cross and his resurrection. The two events dealt Satan double blows which set people free from suffering, sin and death (cf. Heb 2:14-15).

Were the Scribes, whose duty it was to read the Law, study and explain it, obtuse to the ultimate victories of Jesus? Thank God, we're more blessed than they with our faith in and knowledge of his final blows against what St. Paul calls the rulers of darkness. "Finally, grow strong in the Lord, with the strength of his power. Put God's armor on so as to be able to resist the devil's tactics. For it is not against human enemies that we have to struggle, but against the Sovereignties and the Powers who originate the darkness in this world, the spiritual army of evil in the heavens" (Ep 6:10-12).

Blindly the Scribes blaspheme Jesus. They blame him who is God for evil and call him the cause of evil. Jesus' power truly derives from the Spirit of God, as he says, "But if it is through the Spirit of God that I cast devils out, then know that the kingdom of God has overtaken you" (Mt 12:28). No sin, not even blasphemy, is unpardonable, unless the perpetrator is deliberately closed to conversion. The Scribes too are pardonable, and all who charge God with the evil in the world, who feel themselves cursed, by calling upon the name and power of Jesus to heal them. A fact to remember is that divine power is always stronger than the demonic.

The ancient name for Satan was Beelzebul, the prince or leader of an army of demons who could control humans, originally the name of a Philistine god mockingly nicknamed "the lord of the flies."

In 1955, an English novelist or author of fables, William Golding, titled a book *The Lord of the Flies*. It's a book about a bunch of English school boys who, due to an atomic war, a holocaust, are shipped as refugees to an island in the South Seas. They run the island themselves, without chaperones, and attempt to organize into a community effort to find food and shelter, to build and tend a fire signaling for a rescue. But then, like a kingdom or household, they become divided among themselves and eventually turn into killers. Worse yet, a mysterious threat, referred to as "the Thing" which really is Beelzebul or "lord of the flies" appears on a mountain.

Throughout his fable, Golding grapples with the mystery of evil, how it originates, how it surfaces in civilized society, and what to do about it. The boys, innocent to begin with, succumb to evil; gradually their little group disintegrates into animal-like behavior. They represent conservatives, intellectuals and criminals. The democratic society they try to organize demoralizes into a wolf pack. Not only do they lose their innocence, they lose something of their humanity.

Lord of the Flies raises many questions about contemporary morality, but it doesn't have all the answers. Surely evil forces exist and prowl in the world, but are they realities or projections, bogey spirits we invent because of our own evil? Is there really an "unclean spirit," and if so, does it arise from without or from within humanity? Is there evil lurking outside or inside us, or both? For us to shift human guilt to a force from without is an easy ploy. By totally blaming somebody else for it, we excuse ourselves.

Beelzebul is for real. Yet Beelzebul can league with evil *human* spirits, and the two can tempt and prey upon people.

How can we judge evil and good spirits in society? John the apostle replies, "It is not every spirit, my dear people, that you can trust; test them, to see if they come from God . . . You can tell the spirits that come from God by this: every spirit which acknowledges that Jesus the Christ has come in the flesh is from God; but any spirit which will not say this of Jesus (which breaks, splits, or divides him) is not from God, but is the spirit of Antichrist" (1 Jn 4:1-3).

Golding's book offers no satisfactory solution to the problem of evil. How to chain and keep the evil spirit from doing harm isn't to be found in psychology, culture, education, law (evil can use them for its own purpose), nor in common sense. The one and only solution is Christ.

John Milton, the English poet, put it at his literary best: "Leader of their armies bright / Which but the Omnipotent none could have foiled."

32

DIALOGUING WITH GOD

Lk 18:9-14

Ancient Hebrew wisdom was taught in the form of proverbs, which were easier to remember than prosaic statements.
Two of them read as follows: "A man's conduct may strike him
as upright; Yahweh, however, weighs the heart." "He who
conceals his faults will not prosper; he who confesses and
renounces them will find mercy" (Pr 21:2; 28:13). Whether Jesus
had these two proverbs in mind when singling out the Pharisee
and the publican at prayer, we don't know. Anyway, they contain
the truth and wisdom of his words.

To Luke the evangelist, the setting of the gospel of Jesus is
ever important because, for the gospel to be effective for life, it
has to be true to life. Jesus draws his from real Palestinian life:
the house of God, where we overhear two men praying. Their
postures, though not identical with ours, remind us that our
external acts of religion enhance and intensify our internal spirit.
Jesus presents the two to those "who pass themselves off as
virtuous in people's sight" (16:15), while God sees into their
hearts.

The Pharisee assumes a prominent position and raises his
eyes and hands toward heaven. His practice is to pray at mid-
morning and mid-afternoon. His is a prayer of thanksgiving for

127

his good deeds or virtues, though his recital of them contains some odious comparisons of himself with everyone else, particularly the publican. The Hebraic law orders a fast only once a year, on the Day of Atonement, but, supposedly for the conversion of sinners, the Pharisee fasts twice a week, customarily on Mondays and Thursdays. His fast is rather strict, from food *and* drink; the latter is severe for one who lives in a hot, dry climate. And he pays tithes of food and drink on ten percent of his income. Altogether he excels in what Raphael taught to Tobit and Tobias, "Prayer with fasting and alms with right conduct are better than riches with impunity" (Tb 12:8). The Catholic catechism refers to prayer, fasting and almsgiving as three eminently good works. The Pharisee deems himself so well off spiritually that he is not about to exchange places with anybody.

In contrast, the publican doesn't lift his eyes to heaven. He stands in the back with his arms crossed over his chest, the posture of a man who experiences deep, heartfelt remorse. He cries for mercy, a penitential prayer similar to the *Miserere* of the sinful David, "Have mercy on me, O God, in your goodness . . . My sacrifice is this broken spirit, you will not scorn this crushed and broken heart" (Ps 51:7, 17). The reason why he doesn't feel thankful as the Pharisee is that he is (or is taken to be) a swindler, a disreputable fellow, and a social outcast.

As a customs officer he has a poor reputation for collecting taxes from his countrymen while in the employment of the Roman government. The Romans farmed out the tax collection by districts to the highest bidders. They regulated the amount for each district but left it up to the officers to solicit what they could. They could defraud the citizens and draw profit. To make restitution the customs officer had to keep a record of his misdealings and pay one-fifth of his income besides. The publican finds himself in a hopeless situation, broken-hearted, far from God.

What may surprise us is that the Pharisee isn't sinful, nor is he accused of sin, nor is his self-righteous or complacent feeling attributable to all the Pharisees in the time of Jesus. After his conversion, Paul speaks of himself, "I am a Pharisee and the son of Pharisees" (Ac 23:6). Why then doesn't God accept the Pharisee's prayer? Why is the publican able to return home "at rights with God," after humble, appealing prayer, without having made restitution?

Being "at rights with God" is a matter of justification. Is the publican justified simply because he puts faith in prayer? What about the restitution to all the tax payers he defrauded? Faith must go hand in hand with good works. Paul explains the initial value of faith: "If a man has work to show [as did the Pharisee], his wages aren't considered as a favor but as his due; but when a man has nothing to show except faith in the one who justifies sinners, then his faith is considered as justifying him" (Rm 4:4-5). The Pauline doctrine of justification is rooted in Jesus' teaching that faith alone, without good works, without love, can't save.

Why then, since the Pharisee and publican both believe in prayer, does the one find favor with God, the other not? What is faulty about the faith or trust of the Pharisee is that he has too high an opinion of himself, and as a result he trusts less in God than in his own piety. His confidence is misplaced.

Is it true, as is often said, that God answers all prayers, though not always in the way we hope for? Is prayer that lacks the right qualities answerable? A traditional quality of prayer, to be sure, is humility. Jesus presupposes this quality in putting the finishing touch to his story: "For everyone who exalts himself will be humbled, but the man who humbles himself will be exalted." The humbling experience for anyone who prays is to realize that his or her prayer can be found unacceptable and left unanswered.

Yet God undoubtedly listens to prayer. His yes or no to it depends on the disposition of the pray-er. What must God think of trust in one's own piety, self-reliance, self-sufficiency?

The characters of the Pharisee and publican are delineated against the backgrounds of their lives. They pray as they do because that's how they live. In order for them to pray differently, they would have to switch roles in life. That may very well be the meaning Jesus thrusts at us, that we *are* our prayer. Prayer before God, in the house of God, is revealing of our true selves. Whatever there is of fakery, hypocrisy, pride of life, self-reliance, it emerges in prayer. Every true prayer requires something of the publican spirit, "God, be merciful to me, a sinner."

Somehow, overhearing the Pharisee-publican dialogue with God, we're led to evaluate prayer in our own life—such as the prayer of thanksgiving in the life of the Pharisee and those of petition and pardon in the life of the poor publican, and the qualities of prayer—trust and humility.

33

A CAUSE FOR CELEBRATION

Lk 15:11-32

The family affair of the merciful father and his two sons, the one prodigal and the other dutiful, the best known of Jesus' parables because of its human interest and appeal, is often read at the communal celebration of the sacrament of reconciliation. It reads like a passage out of a diary, depicting three episodes. The first is when the younger son is seen at home asking his father for his share of the family fortune, then abroad, and finally back home again. The changes of scene and mood are rather dramatic, freeing our imagination and emotions. We come to feel like friends of the family.

The younger son is restless at home with his father, awaiting his share of the family inheritance. The older son, apparently, isn't present for the departure of his brother but learns of it later. The younger son is single, of a marriageable age—between 18 and 20. At home he has a livelihood, but not enough to his satisfaction. He feels a spirit of independence, grown-up, and since there doesn't seem to be much opportunity for advancement at home he intends to go abroad into the Greco-Roman world. Like many sons and daughters nowadays, he wants to launch a career away from the old hometown.

The father can hand down the family belongings in two

131

ways. Either by means of a will, and then the sons will have to wait till his death, or by gift during his lifetime. The father divides the property but retains the profit or interest from it, the usufruct, which is available to the sons only after his death. The older son will get full possession of his share eventually, the capital and the interest.

The younger son, inexperienced in the ways of the Greco-Roman world yet attracted to them, has his fling, wasting his wealth and himself on wine, women and song. Before he realizes it, the bon vivant loses even a livelihood. He personally experiences the truth of the proverbs: "The patron of harlots fritters his wealth away," and "The drunkards and gluttons impoverish themselves" (Pr 29:3; 23:21). He goes from feast to famine. To stave off starvation, he has to hire himself out to a farmer to feed his pigs and live with them, with unclean animals which the Hebrew people think unfit for the worship of God and therefore unfit for themselves (Lv 11:7). He is forced to eat their food without permission when no one offers him any other. He suffers from the wages of sin.

At times sin is so habit-forming, so much of an addiction, that the sinner is unable to free himself from it; he feels himself trapped in its consequences. In effect, they may bring him back to his senses, as they do for the younger son. He remembers his happy past, which also helps to bring about his conversion. He turns away from his recent evil and unhappy state, even though he has no further claim to anything back home. He's willing to confess his sinfulness and, hopefully, be received as a hired hand.

Seen at a distance from his home, he already is taking a step along the way of his conversion. His reconversion points to the fact that once fallen into sin, only a little good effort will turn us away from evil and set us back on the right track. No need to grovel in sin. Stepping accidentally into a mud puddle doesn't necessarily keep us standing in it.

Upon his arrival home, the prodigal son is showered with affection and mercy. His father kisses him—a sign of mercy, just as King David kissed Absalom, his belligerent son (2 S 14:33). The son is wrapped in a robe of distinction, a ring is slipped on his finger to symbolize authority, as Pharaoh put a ring on Joseph's finger in Egypt (1 Mc 6:15; Gn 41:42), and sandals are put on his feet to bestow a freedom no barefooted slave has. Last of all, he's feted at a banquet, with music and dance, to make him feel at home again at the family table. The feast of a fatted calf is so rare a treat that it turns the eye of the older brother green with envy. After all, he had helped in fattening it.

The older son, so obedient and dutiful, who remains at his father's side—possibly in his father's declining years when he's unable to run his estate—is angered by all the festivity which he thinks the younger brother is undeserving of. He refuses to join in the celebration, so that the father has to reproach his firstborn son to whom so much of the inheritance is due (Dt 21:17). He acts like the Pharisees and Scribes who accuse Jesus of wrong company-keeping and of dining with sinners.

The return of the younger son and the protest of the older both elicit the same explanation from the father: "This son of mine was dead and has come back to life; he was lost and is found." The return to God from the death of sin is a spiritual resurrection to life. The sinful son is a lost sheep that is found.

This triple scene with its sin, sorrow and protest, ends happily, arousing a sense of joy. We're the more joyful when somebody close and dear to us recuperates from a sinful way of life, than when somebody like the older son stays faithful to his father and pouts.

The father images God in his loving kindness toward wayward sinners. The divine mercy is a bit of the good news Jesus proclaims to us, and the answer to his critics. In narrating this story of the compassionate, merciful father, Jesus represents his Father.

How often have we heard it? Seventy times seven? But hearing it this time over, the thought comes to me that one character is missing from it—the mother of the family. Her absence seems all the more poignant in our Lord's time when motherhood was rated so highly in society. Perhaps this young man's mother had died when he was very small. Could that explain his actions? Family life is no more matriarchal now than it was patriarchal then, in the life and times of Jesus. Mothers celebrate the return of an unfaithful son no less than fathers do.

In this connection, I can't help but recall Monica, the mother of Augustine, who prayed long for his conversion and then, before her death, saw her prayers come true. The divine pity or compassion for the sinner, flowing through the heart whether of a father or of a mother, always calls for a celebration in the family.

34

SPIRITUAL COMBAT

Lk 14:31-32

Kings in the Old Testament were ever ready for war, even annually. Thus the king whom Jesus speaks about is ready for war. But before attempting a defense he pauses to size up his enemy. Between himself and the hostile king there is no balance of power which would help to ward off attack. Outnumbered twice over, military prudence dictates that, rather than enter into a war of attrition, the king come to terms of peace with the enemy and surrender unconditionally.

It paid the military leaders of Israel in the past to check over both their own strength and that of the enemy. When they went about the conquest of the promised land of Canaan, they had to muster offensive and defensive means of combat. But Israel had the assurance that the conquest was a "war of Yahweh," that he alone was its strength. Israel had on its hands both a physical and, to boot, a spiritual struggle against idolatry. It was and still is much easier to calculate the means necessary for physical combat than for spiritual—against the forces of evil.

These are the enemy the kingdom of God has to contend with, and against such Jesus wants his disciples to prepare themselves. A careful assessment of strength is called for, a test of oneself.

The conditions for combat are so tough that we shouldn't respond to the recruitment by Christ without due reflection. His call of a disciple is to total self-surrender. A disciple may be asked to renounce marriage, money, possessions, life itself. The spiritual combat permits no time for detente, for relaxation from the fight.

Jesus spoke about the king on the march to war at a time when he himself was on his way to crucifixion, just as his enemies began to gather their forces together for the kill. He forecasted that discipleship entails suffering and dying, a share in his death as well as in his life.

The crucifixion he had to endure involved him at once in both the political and the religious worlds. Many in his time, as later in the discipleship of Paul, behaved as "the enemies of the cross of Christ" (Ph 3:18). To some of his contemporaries Jesus appeared to be a political and religious revolutionary. Martyrs, too, the American, Chinese, Japanese, and African, though they died in a spirit of faith, were often held to be political enemies.

Is it possible to engage in religious combat without political entanglements? Martyrdom isn't death by assassination. Nor is it death for the sake of an ideology. To die patriotically for one's country isn't quite the same as dying for one's God.

War against the forces of evil is a continual contention in the Christian life. The Church is in a state of holy war to establish the kingdom of heaven, for "the kingdom of heaven has been subjected to violence" (Mt 11:12). Our "enemy the devil is prowling round like a roaring lion" (1 P 5:8). "For it is not against human enemies that we have to struggle, but against the Sovereignties and the Powers who originate the darkness of this world, the spiritual army of evil in the heavens" (Ep 6:12).

For a militant Christian the struggle is human, the sustaining power is God. "Grow strong in the Lord, with the strength of his power," wrote Paul to the Ephesians (6:10). "That is why you must rely on God's armor, or you will not be able to put up any resistance when the worst happens, or have enough resources to hold your ground" (6:13). God's armor is spiritual for a spiritual struggle: "Faith and love for a *breastplate*, and the hope of *salvation* for a *helmet*" (1 Th 5:8).

Ordinarily, physical warfare, at the cost of many lives and huge devastation, may result in a peace which is nothing more than a temporary absence of conflict. But spiritual warfare is the price we pay for peace of heart. And without it no other peace in life can prevail. Spiritually speaking, we maintain peace in ourselves only by preparing for war; the preparation is ongoing—not simply to become a disciple but to *remain* one. The ten persecutions in the history of the early Church saw many Christians fall away from the Church, unable to remain disciples of Christ.

The military role of ancient Israelite kings was to equip an army and prepare for war; the royal role of the Christian is to follow Christ the King on the way of the cross. Although declared king of the Jews during the crucifixion, Jesus was truly the king of the universe on the cross because there he defeated the universal enemy, evil itself. Thomas a Kempis wrote in his *Imitation of Christ* that "in the cross is protection from enemies . . . in the cross is strength of mind." The *Imitation* prods the reader: "How is it that you look for another way than this, the royal way of the holy cross?" (Bk II, Ch. 12).

The man who popularized the phrase, "the cost of discipleship," was the Lutheran minister Dietrich Bonhoeffer. He was born February 4, 1906, in Breslau and brought up in Berlin, the child of a well-known family of royal aristocratic blood, with a long tradition. He titled one of his books with the German *Nachfolge*, published in 1937, the literal English translation of which should read, "The Following (of Christ)." In it he wrote, "When Christ calls a man, he bids him come and die." Eight years after its German publication, Bonhoeffer exemplified the essence of discipleship with the last deed of his life.

Hitler came to power in 1933. Bonhoeffer foresaw that the Nazi party would threaten Germany and the Christian way of life, and became a leading member of the opposition to it. Asked, "What will you do when war comes," he replied, "I shall pray to Christ to give me the power not to take up arms." Bonhoeffer went the royal way of the cross in the concentration camp at Flossenburg: he was hanged April 9, 1945.

Not all disciples of Christ are drafted into this kind of combat—physical martyrdom, the costliest of graces. But we're all taught to estimate our strength and to realize that for spiritual combat we need the strength of Christ.

35

HIGH RANK

Lk 14:7-11

For dignitaries and celebrities at a banquet or formal dinner, say, at the White House, attendance is only by invitation and seating is likely to be marked by place cards according to social rank, dignity, relationship, or friendship. Unless they misread or mistake their places at table, guests have no opportunity to maneuver into high-ranking places. Even the society news editor, reporting such a social event, would list the guests by rank.

But in the time of Jesus, the practice among the Pharisees and Scribes was something else (cf. Lk 20:46). He couldn't help but notice how they vied for the places of honor at the meal he was invited to by one of the leading Pharisees. They could save themselves the embarrassment, he remarked, by taking lower places at the table and then, by invitation of their host, move up higher. Customarily the Pharisees and Scribes pridefully came last to a party and sought out, or expected to be escorted to, the first places at table. They were a knowledgeable clique who liked to engage in mealtime conversation about the Law. They felt sure of the first places at the table in God's kingdom.

The ranks in God's kingdom, however, may be altogether different from what they are at social events. In fact, Jesus was enunciating a first principle of the spiritual life: "Everyone who exalts himself will be humbled, and the man who humbles himself will be exalted."

Moreover, he laid down a rule of table etiquette, gently forewarning the Pharisees, Scribes, and all lucky enough to get the lowest place at the heavenly feast. His word contained some proverbial wisdom: "In the presence of the king do not give yourself airs, do not put yourself where the great are standing; better to be invited, 'Come up here' than be humiliated in the presence of the prince" (Pr 25:6-7).

This humiliation-exaltation principle blends a wise saying with the course of events in his own life. For him to have taken a high-ranking position at a Pharisee's table and then be asked to remove himself was out of character. He lived what he preached. As a teacher who spoke spontaneously out of the experiences of his life, Jesus was truly a man "gentle and humble of heart" (Mt 11:29). Eventually, we know, Jesus personally experienced the most profound humiliation-exaltation in his passage from the crucifixion to the resurrection to the ascension.

"The God of the humble" (Jdt 9:11) inculcates a spirit of humility in his followers. Humility is an old-fashioned term, very much down-to-earth, but for want of something better— unless it be "sincerity"—it will have to do.

Guests who imitate the God of the humble will assume prominent positions at table in his kingdom to come. He prefers the humble or poor who submit themselves to his will and are thoughtful of others. They go by the name of *anawim*, the remnant of Israel.

Admittedly humility is a dish not easy to digest. Hubris can't stomach it. And all the savory explanations of it in the world doesn't make it more palatable. Because God seats himself with the humble and lowly, he must intend them for our company too. Adopting the Pharisaic attitude of looking out for only high places in public, and bringing more judgment upon others below them in social standing, are hardly ways of learning humility. Even social climbers may be stepping up through subtle pride.

Self-knowledge, which also nourishes humility, can scarcely be imbibed like instant tea or coffee. The discovery of the true self may be likened to a full course dinner. The distinction of the false self from the true is more like recognizing one's place at table. The Pharisees may have been more knowledgeable about the Law than they were about themselves. Apparently they hadn't yet filled themselves at the banquet before Jesus gave them a course in humility.

He did the same for his disciples at the Last Supper. They had been disputing among themselves about who was the greatest in their company. The greatest, he said, weren't the guests but the servants (cf. Lk 22:24, 26-27). He made it plain during his ministry that "the Son of Man came not to be served but to serve" (Mt 20:28).

Jesus humbles himself before his guests at the table of his word and sacrament. His table serves humility rather than feeds pride.

T.S. Eliot wrote a free verse and poetic comedy about a sophisticated society that moved from one party to another. *The Cocktail Party*, as he named it, seems to be saying that human society tends to act like one continual cocktail party. What are the implications?

A character in the play, Edward, can't answer questions about his wife Lavinia because she has left him, and he's too embarrassed to confess the fact to a guest. The guest observes that "this would be all to the good—that surviving humiliation is an experience of incalculable value."

The guest turns out to be a psychiatrist to whom Edward confides in conversation, "But I am obsessed by the thought of my own significance." To which the psychiatrist responds: "Precisely. And I could make you feel important, / And you would imagine it a marvelous cure; . . . Half of the harm that is done in this world / Is due to people who want to feel important. / They don't mean to do harm—but the harm does not interest them. / Or they do not see it, or they justify it / Because they are absorbed in the endless struggle / To think well of themselves."

A second character, Celia, finds it humiliating that she has pursued a wrong dream rather than the real goal of life. Edward believes she has no reason to feel humiliated. She replies: "Oh, don't think that *you* can humiliate me! / Humiliation—it's something I've done to myself. / I am not sure even that you seem real enough / To humiliate me. . . ."

Later, as a missionary to Kinkanja, a fictional country, Celia "must have been crucified / Very near an ant-hill." The news of her humiliation-exaltation finish to life stuns the guests at a cocktail party.

36

THE MIRROR OF TRUTH

Lk 6:39-42;   Mt 15:14

"Can one blind man guide another? The disciple is not superior to his teacher; . . . Why do you observe the splinter in your brother's eye and never notice the plank in your own?" (Lk 6:39-41). Maxims such as these in the teaching of Jesus are strung together by the biblical author into pearl necklaces of wisdom, truths to live by.

And truths, simple and plain, to ponder. They are miniatures, images of Jesus himself, who is the way, the truth, and the life. Blind leaders, like the Pharisees to whom Jesus makes reference, are bound to lead their fellow Hebrews astray. Jesus replaces these blind religious leaders with his own disciples who know and follow him in his way of life.

Without much discipline, disciples (literally, learners) are not about to surpass their teachers. They will have to do their utmost to match their teachers. The disciple who intends to excel his teacher has to make it on his own, by his own effort. In the Christian life, the disciple will have enough to do to imitate Jesus the Teacher.

The maxims, though addressed to Jesus' disciples, may as well have been spoken to all hearers of his word—the Pharisees, his rivals in religion, and the crowd at large. How so? Because, in

143

the imagery of the splinter and the plank, Jesus doesn't have the literal meaning of "brother" in mind. The Greek term for brother is *adelphos*, which refers not only to a blood-brother but to one's "neighbor" in its most comprehensive sense.

How is it possible to detect the splinter in a neighbor's eye without noticing the plank in one's own, since a plank is so much more of an obstruction to vision than a splinter? How can one be more plainly spoken?

Plank or splinter are figures of speech for fault-finding, which is forbidden by the eighth commandment—to bear false witness against one's neighbor. Did the founders of our nation contradict this commandment with the first amendment of the Constitution of the U.S.: "Congress shall make no law . . . abridging freedom of speech, or of the press"?

False witness, a social evil, so human, so widespread, can grow into enormous proportions—the defamation of character or libel (if published). Character flaws proliferate, faults and weaknesses seem to appear larger in others than in ourselves, not because they *are* larger in others but because we may magnify them with imaginings larger than reality.

The splinter is a suspicion, based on slight evidence, of evil. To suspect a neighbor isn't nearly as bad as judging him/her rashly. A plank is rash judgment. Rash judgment passes a far worse verdict of guilt than suspicion, without sufficient reason. In psychiatry, fault-finding is labeled "paranoia." It is a serious psychic tendency to project our personal problems on others whom we blame for them.

Fault-finding has nothing to do with the correction or discipline which parents, teachers, or preachers have to exercise on children and youngsters, even adults, when they get out of hand. The motive behind such parental, neighborly, friendly correction or discipline is love. Love wants nothing more than to draw the best conduct from others, to encourage the true gifts others have in themselves, so that they can use them to serve their neighbors, achieve a good Christian name in society, and bear witness to Christ. For parents, teachers and preachers to educate God's children in Christ-like ways of life is to leave them with a heritage of far greater value than property or wealth.

The mental and/or verbal attack on a neighbor by fault-finding Jesus designates as hypocrisy, which is a lie, a form of blindness (the term for it in the gospel of John). Leveled at the Pharisee, the cry "Hypocrite!" is a bitter offense. A hypocrite finds the eighth commandment of God a stumbling block (Si 32:15), contrary to his/her pretense of thinking himself/herself better than others. Narrow-sightedly and narrow-mindedly, criticism betrays a lack of spiritual honesty (cf. 1 P 2:2), and leaves no peace of mind.

Only the removal of the plank from the eye will restore the clear vision which sees the goodness and kindness of the Creator mirrored in his creation. God himself looks to his creation and finds it to be good, and his human creature very good. He would have each of us develop and keep a good self-image. With plank in eye, we fail to perceive ourselves as being images and likenesses of the Creator. Consequently the divine in us appears as in an imperfect distorted mirror. Everything looking awry, if not false and ugly.

In the children's fairy tale of Snow White and the Seven Dwarfs, truth shines forth and speaks from a magical mirror. So when the queen stepmother of Snow White gazes on herself in the magical mirror and asks, "Mirror, mirror on the wall / Who is fairest of us all?" the glass answers truthfully, "Thou, queen, art fairest of them all," because the queen stepmother is truly beautiful.

But as Snow White grows up, seven years old, white as snow, red as blood, and black as ebony, she's fairer than the queen stepmother herself. On consulting the glass again, the latter is told, "Queen, you are full fair, 'tis true, / But Snow White fairer is than you." As a matter of fact, Snow White is a thousand times fairer. The Seven Dwarfs who find her in their home, comment too, "Oh, what a lovely child she is!"

The queen stepmother, unable to tolerate a rival to her beauty, turns pale with rage and envy. Spite and malice drive her to plot the murder of Snow White, and she finally succeeds in poisoning her with an apple. A prince comes along, finds and falls in love with the beautiful Snow White who even in death remains beautiful. As the prince lifts her up, the poisoned bite of apple falls from her lips and Snow White comes to life again. The queen stepmother hears about it, is choked with passion, falls ill and dies.

The splinter and the plank analogy has a fairy tale quality about it. At the same time, it mirrors the real life of those who find fault with creation. It would have been useful to the queen stepmother whose vision of Snow White was distorted by anger and envy, spite and malice. The mirror, not the eye of the beholder, facilitates the removal of a plank.

37

THE DANGER OF RELAPSE

Mt 12:43-45;   Lk 11:24-26

The two locales where the evil spirits traditionally hang out are the waterless countryside (wilderness or desert) and the home left empty and clean. The two are very real to Palestinian settlers whose dry land borders fertile areas.

The "unclean spirit" is restless, full of the wanderlust. Can "it" ever settle down? Will it ever take a breather away from bad company? Instead of setting up house for itself, it returns to its former hangout with "seven other spirits more evil than itself." They're impersonal but not neutral toward good or evil. They're demons. And yet their leader speaks personally, "I will return to the home I came from."

We're not informed *where* the demonic leader goes off to collect seven others. That there *are* others around isn't left open to question. Spirits who have Satan for their leader are able to roam over the world to exert power and influence over God's people. They're invisible to bodily mortals, unlikely to reveal themselves as evil but ambitious to alienate people from God once and for all. The Bible portrays them as gods of this world (2 Cor 4:4), or as spiritual powers, or as world elements, or as elemental principles of the world, or as evil powers that control

147

the world. Whatever their powers, they leave humans in the dark and remain a threat to world stability and peace.

The first public struggle Jesus had was with Satan in his own environment, the desert. His last public act was to defeat Satan by dying on the cross, under a human verdict. His victory on the cross helped to realize God's kingdom but didn't deal a definitive blow to demonic spirits. They still have some power of evil over the world and won't lose it finally till God's kingdom comes to full reality.

That's why no "home" should be left open, unprotected, or readied for an uninvited guest. A demonic spirit once expelled from a place, may return when the owner isn't on guard against intruders, or has no alarm system. Otherwise the owner may find himself in a predicament worse than before.

Now, demons prefer to dwell in human beings who are kindred spirits, rather than in hell. The human heart is much more to their liking than any home kept neat and tidy, with a comfortable sofa in the parlor and a TV set with cable hookup.

The return of the evil spirit signals a relapse. Relapse into sin or into the power of evil need not always follow a first invasion. In saying "that is what will happen to this evil generation," Jesus is taking a shot against the Scribes and Pharisees who misrepresent Israel. They help to create a pseudo-Israel of backsliders and recidivists. They're not resolved upon real, heartfelt repentance.

Jesus' warning applies to some extent, in a small way at least, to all backsliders or recidivists. After a sincere confession of our sinfulness and guilt, we resolve to amend our evil ways, but occasionally fall back into them anyway. We're ever needful of the powerful, merciful word of Jesus that drives away demonic spirits, seven of them in all.

A symbolic number, seven in this context suggests all that is evil, every type of demonic attraction and every wicked deed. Though, of itself, evil is never attractive, it always appears in the guise of good. If we expect to see demonic spirits with seven ugly, hideous faces, as they have been depicted in art and literature, we will be hoodwinked.

Happily for our sake, we have been tipped off about how these "seven other spirits" may possibly return to us. Experience with evil temptations has taught us to beware of them. They continue to threaten us, and we have to contend with them every day in order to be faithful Christians. By name, they're the seven capital sins: pride, envy, anger, sloth, greed or avarice, gluttony and lust. The first three are of a more spiritual nature, the latter three more fleshly, with sloth lying in between, prone to relapse into the other six, unable to rescue us from the rest.

Geoffrey Chaucer, the fourteenth century English poet, at the end of his *Canterbury Tales*, has his parson preach to the pilgrims—people very much like ourselves, with the same human strengths and weaknesses—about the seven capital sins. For over forty-five years, Chaucer had observed men and women, each endowed with individualizing traits embodying a cross-section of English life. And he writes of them as pilgrims to the favorite medieval shrine of Canterbury.

Among the pilgrims, the monk starts his tale by speaking of Lucifer: "From high degree yet fell he for his sin / Down into Hell, and he lies yet therein." But the monk's confinement of Lucifer to hell doesn't keep the parson from preaching about the capital sins at the end of the pilgrimage. "They are," he says, "the principal sins; they are leashed together, but they are different in their ways. Now they are called principal sins because they are the chief sins and the trunk from which branch all others. And the root of these seven sins is pride, which is the general root of all evils; for from this root spring certain branches. . . ."

The parson ("To lead folk into Heaven by stress / Of good example was his busyness") is asked by the host of the pilgrimage to be brief in his explanation, but he is in fact rather long-winded. Not only does he describe the seven capital sins at length; he lists the remedies for each of them. The person who speaks for Chaucer knows his spiritual theology. He hardly misses a trick or ruse the evil spirits may try. Inevitably he shows how the devil has his hands in the spread of evil: five fingers in gluttony and five in lust, he says, for they are "such close cousins that oftentimes they will not be separated." He studiously warns that the destructive forces may come from without, like intruders into a home, but they seek to lodge within the heart, where they do the most damage.

Students of demonology may hesitate to identify the "seven other spirits" with the seven capital sins, but Chaucer is wise in instructing and cautioning against relapse into them in the pilgrimage through life.

38

THE COURT OF FINAL APPEAL

Mt 25:31-46

The scene of the last judgment lies beyond our imagination. Were we to try to conjure it up, most likely it would lean
toward a courtroom scene such as we see in our legal system. In
it, God the Father is seated in the role of judge, Jesus his Son
assumes the part of an associate judge, the twelve apostles line
up as jurors in a jury box, and the angels stand by as clerks or
executioners of the sentence. In reality, our scene-setting is far
removed from the end of the world and the final judgment
which Matthew describes at the conclusion of his gospel. Aside
from all his figures of speech, the ultimate truth is contained in
our profession of faith: "Thence he (Christ) shall come to judge
the living and the dead."

The Matthean description has several points of interest
open to interpretation: a panorama, an assembly of peoples, and
some standards of judgment. The roles of Jesus, the central
figure in the judgment scene, are set in relief.

His first title and role is that of the Son of Man. Though
borrowed from the Old Testament, especially from the prophets
Ezekiel and Daniel, he uses it of himself in delineating his
human life. The human Christ suffers the humiliation of the
cross, to experience afterward the exaltation of the resurrection,

151

to return in glory at the end of the world when he will execute judgment. Human as he is and remains, he's the better judge in our case. Of this fact the apostle Paul never loses sight, even to the extent of seeing the judgment as a law court of Christ, and each of us will get what he deserves for the things he did in the body, good and bad" (2 Cor 5:10).

In the Matthean description, Christ keeps switching roles: shepherd, then king, and finally Lord. His appearance is before a vast assembly—the whole people of God, including nonbelievers and non-Christians who have never heard explicitly of God or of Christ. How are they to be judged, by what standards? Is it fair to them to be judged by the same standards as believers and Christians?

Jesus doesn't hold it against nonbelievers and non-Christians if through no fault of their own they lack explicit faith in him. They're judged on the basis of the light they have received in this life and on their works of mercy and justice. Their light may be no more illuminating than their conscience, energized by good will. Jesus asks basically as much of them as of anyone, namely, good works performed for the benefit of the hungry, thirsty, stranger, naked, sick, prisoners—in a word, for the poor and needy. The traditional corporal and spiritual works of mercy rate high in his judgment.

They are a decisive factor, pro and con, in the final judgment of humankind, bearing more heavily on what is left undone. The sins he takes principally into account are the sins of omission—our failure to serve the poor in the world who represent him, and he in turn decides against all who neglect them (cf. Dt 15:9).

Jesus, the Lord of history is, though hidden and disguised, identifiable with all people, even (more challengingly to our perception) with the least of them. The Lord judges the treatment given to them as to himself, even if one may not realize that it is being given to him personally living incognito in the poor and needy. The final scene goes to show that the Lord is guided in his rule of the world by the same two standards: mercy and justice.

Herein lies the difference in judgment between the Old and New Testaments. In the Old, the basis of judgment was one's conduct toward God, prescribed in the covenant and Law. But in the new the basis of judgment is one's attitude toward Jesus himself—the test case, the model for all people, believers and unbelievers.

The virtuous who did works of mercy and justice but inquire, "*When* did we see you . . .?" might disclaim any recognition of Jesus in the person of the poor and needy. Even so, he examines their past attitude. Have they had any intention of performing good works with strings attached? If so, they may already have had their reward: the final rewards are for the unselfish, the spontaneous, the sincere.

Then Jesus, donning the role of the shepherd, separates all those assembled—a "mixed" flock, the good and the bad, as a shepherd separates sheep from goats. Sheep and goats are kept together in Palestine till nightfall, when the sheep are left in the open air but the goats have to be kept warm indoors, in the cool of the night.

The king characteristically pronounces judgment, which Jesus does by dividing the assembly to the right and to the left of himself. On the right the people are invited into the kingdom of his Father; the people on the left have to depart from him into everlasting fire.

Elusive as the last judgment is to our imaginations, Matthew pictures some truths about it that are inescapable: the roles Christ plays in it, and the bit parts we as a people have in it. One truth is that in all justice we can't leave the final judgment to any human tribunal. Christ in his several roles is the only world court with unfailing judgment. All other judgment seats have only a provisional and passing place in human history.

The single standard of judgment Christ employs reverts to the commandment of love that he laid down for us, a commandment embodied in his own life, mysteriously hidden in him as in the poor and needy. No one can lay any claim against him, or defer to a higher court, or postpone a verdict indefinitely by legal entanglements. He can always say, "You did it to me," or "You neglected to do it to me." His spiritual identification with the poor and needy is revealed as never before in the last judgment. Only then will there appear, for all to see, believers and unbelievers alike, the definitive people of God his Father.

EPILOGUE

G.K. Chesterton, the British journalist turned novelist, has the leading character in *The Poet and the Lunatics: Episodes in the Life of Gabriel Gale* say, "I doubt whether any truth can be told except in parable." His statement, typically Chestertonian, can hardly be more relevant than to the concrete, lifelike, practical truth found in Jesus' parables. They are true to his life, who is Truth incarnate. Surely the parable is as true as any philosophical, abstract truth, though untypical of the storyteller and possibly exercising a greater influence on life.

Jesus had many things to say in parables, but not everything. Toward the end of the gospel of John, in the farewell discourse to his disciples, he remarked, "I still have many things to say to you but they would be too much for you now" (16:12). Jesus didn't leave his remark dangling in the air nor did he leave his disciples in suspense. He went on to say, "But when the Spirit of truth comes he will lead you to the complete truth . . . and he will tell you of the things to come" (16:13). The "complete truth" was too much for the disciples to bear at the time. The "things to come" consisted of the final events in the life of Jesus, to the meaning of which the Spirit was to guide the disciples. The Church today believes it is still under the guidance of the Spirit. It hasn't yet arrived at the complete truth; it still faces "things to come."

155

Jesus' parables aren't just things of the past. The truths they teach were put into practice in his life, were assimilated into the life of the early Church, and are to be part and parcel of the life of each of us as Christians. We are sequels to the parables. Jesus lived them once; we are to relive them now. It is in this sense true to say, "We shall not easily exhaust their meaning" (C.H. Dodd). They are to be found "retold" in the life story each of us has to relate.

Storytelling must never come to an end in the Christian life, not simply because it tickles the fancy and holds the attention. Rather because it helps us to answer the questions of life which the parables put to us. Each storyteller has a point of view, an eye for seeing things aright, getting the hang of some truth, getting a fix on the goal of life. Every Christian story reflects the parables of Jesus in the way that they turn out. We Christians are mirrored in his word.

INDEX